Carolyn Mary Kleefeld

VISIONS FROM BIG SUR

This catalog has been published to accompany the exhibition, *Carolyn Mary Kleefeld: Visions from Big Sur,* organized by the Frederick R. Weisman Museum of Art, Pepperdine University.

Frederick R. Weisman Museum of Art
Pepperdine University
September 13 — December 14, 2008

Frederick R. Weisman Museum of Art
Pepperdine University
24255 Pacific Coast Highway
Malibu, CA 90263

Catalog designed by University Communications, Pepperdine University
Art Director: Gayle Wheatley
Production Manager: Jill McWilliams
Catalog printed by Colourcraft Printing, Culver City, CA
Typeset in Trebuchet

ISBN 1-882705-07-6 *Carolyn Mary Kleefeld: Visions from Big Sur*

Opposite: *Goddess Wearing the Mountain,* 1999, oil on canvas, 24 x 18 inches
Cover: *Heart Grotto,* 2006, (detail) oil on canvas, 48 x 60 inches

Carolyn Mary Kleefeld
VISIONS FROM BIG SUR

Michael Zakian
Frederick R. Weisman Museum of Art
Pepperdine University

From Carolyn Kleefeld's home in Big Sur, nature appears as a mysterious and primal force.

Introduction

This exhibition presents the first full-scale overview of the visual art of Carolyn Mary Kleefeld. It covers twenty-five years, from 1983 to 2008, and includes drawings and paintings in all media, ranging from ink and watercolor to acrylic and oil. Retrospective might be a more accurate term, but it is difficult to capture in a single exhibition or catalog the broad and diverse production of this creative individual. Kleefeld began her adult creative life as a poet in the 1970s. Although she had used drawing and painting as an outlet for her thoughts since childhood, she did not fully immerse herself in visual art as a key part of her life's work until after 1980, when she moved to her current home in Big Sur.

The title of the exhibition, "Visions from Big Sur," may suggest a collection of picturesque scenes of the California coast. Kleefeld paints something more fabulous. As she once explained, she lives on an isolated cliff, high above the Pacific Ocean, in order to better experience the full range of nature's wonders:

> We are living 500 feet above the sea, with a 360-degree view. This serves to keep a lid off our heads. The beauty is a never-ending, changing spectacle. We receive the winds from every direction, which can be quite a challenge to live with. The wildly divergent energies, forces of the "dragon's crown" where I live, are all translated into my art through the instrument of myself in concert with it all.[1]

Kleefeld is a spiritual artist. Her concerns lie not with the material and worldly but with what lies within. She firmly believes in a transcendent reality which unifies and gives meaning to the phenomenal world. For her, this larger spirit or order is seen around us every day but is overlooked by most people. It is found in eternally recurring forms or universal images known as archetypes. It appears in coincidences or chance similarities, which we refer to as moments of synchronicity. It also appears in the deep patterns of human thought, which mirror a greater intelligence beyond us. Aldous Huxley, an author Kleefeld greatly admires, used the term "Perennial Philosophy" to refer to this recurrence of religious and philosophical insights that cross epochs and cultures.[2]

To capture these insights, Kleefeld lets herself function as an "instrument" or mediator of nature. Rather than emphasize the role of the self, she prefers to function as a neutral conduit. In this way she serves as a receptor of deep impressions and meaningful truths. As she explained, "It's more like I become the empty canvas, empty mind, and in becoming one with the atomistic energies that be, these energies, this consciousness, uses my nervous system for its translation."[3]

Some may ask: why take a look at the art of Carolyn Kleefeld now? It is because her work offers a message that is particularly timely. Her worldview emphasizes a respect for all living creatures and an openness to primal natural forces, as a model for integration in our fragmented modern world. The perspective that formed her aesthetic was shaped by a number of cultural forces that converged in California in the 1970s. The rise of the Women's Movement encouraged women to find their own voices. The popularity of Jungian and Humanistic Psychology emphasized the integrity of the autonomous individual. These thinkers placed an emphasis on creativity as a positive human force. Also at that time, many people questioned the materialist base of Western culture and looked for alternatives in Eastern philosophies and religions. The ethos of the time advocated a natural path as a way to regain a sense of individual and social balance. Today, as we begin the 21st century with global warming and shortages of oil and food, these issues are crucial once again.

Carolyn Kleefeld drew upon the intellectual sources of her time, weaving connections between philosophy, psychology, science, and literature into a personal and unique synthesis. As she said,

> Being an artist, I am the translator of my experience and thus am the author of my life. Since each of us experiences something in our own unique way, everything we create is essentially autobiographical. I am at once the tool, and the work. The universe is strumming the strings of my nervous system and I record the songs.[4]

The works in this exhibition should be thought of as songs and poems given visual form. Her paintings serve as a model and provide inspiration to others who seek a similar message of liberation and wholeness.

---

1 "Singing Songs of Ecstasy with Carolyn Mary Kleefeld," in David Jay Brown and Rebecca McClen Novick, *Mavericks of the Mind: Conversations for the New Millennium* (Freedom, CA: The Crossing Press, 1993), 163–4.

2 Aldous Huxley, *The Perennial Philosophy* (New York: Harper & Brothers, 1945).

3 *Mavericks of the Mind,* 168.

4 *Mavericks of the Mind,* 160.

Carolyn Kleefeld on her balcony overlooking the south coast of Big Sur.

Carolyn Mary Kleefeld: the Artist and Her Life

We are nature's forces translating, in human terms, our existence. Art is my bridge of translation. That is why art is the "international language," as it has the myriad tongues of its artists' voices.
—Carolyn Mary Kleefeld[1]

Let art sound like a fairy tale and be at home everywhere. Let it work with good and evil as do the eternal powers. And let it be a holiday, a change of atmosphere and point of view, a transfer to another world which presents a diverting spectacle so that they may return to everyday life with renewed vitality.
—Paul Klee[2]

In 1980 Carolyn Mary Kleefeld left her home in Malibu and her life in Southern California to move to Big Sur. It was the start of a new chapter of her life. Kleefeld was raised in Los Angeles and came of age in Beverly Hills. She grew up in a culture that emphasized competition, achievement, and materialism—a world that was seductive but superficial. Moving allowed her to renew her energy and create a new life closer to her inner values. Big Sur provided her with a deep connection to the natural world and a strong sense of what was true and real.

Living in Big Sur also allowed Kleefeld to further explore her creative potential. Instinctively and independently, she came to share the vision of the pioneering modernist Paul Klee. He called for an art that was magical and spiritual, filled with the wonders of everyday life. It was a passionate art, drawing upon profound emotions and articulating our wildest dreams as well as our most primal fears, but always presenting these insights in the form of a fantastic vision. It was an art, in short, that stemmed from the depths of soul. Kleefeld also believed that art was a way of translating deep inner truths. As an artist, she sees herself as a conduit, as a means of sharing this marvelous gift of creative insight.

Big Sur offered the ideal opportunity to nurture and explore the inner spirit. Located on a remote stretch of the central California coast, this rural and isolated region affords a rare retreat from the trials of modern life. Although her home sits on a promontory with picturesque views, she did not select it for its scenic beauty. Rather, she was drawn to this place intuitively because it offers a direct experience of the wilderness as a primal force. The visual stimulation of Big Sur inspired an innate response in shapes and colors. As she explained, "My painting and drawing, being visual, are pre-lingual."[3] Reacting to nature on a sensuous, instinctual level prompted primal aesthetic reflections.

She joined the ranks of a number of poets, writers, and artists who found Big Sur to be an environment conducive for creating their art. Raw and unadorned, it lacks the artifice that spoils much of contemporary society. Among the first artists of note to move to the region was poet Robinson Jeffers who settled in Carmel, north of Big Sur, in 1913. There he lived in close harmony with nature, an experience which shaped his epic, narrative verse. Most famously, Henry Miller moved to Big Sur proper in the 1940s and became a symbol of the intrepid writer who rejects the insincere posturing of modern life. He helped create the image of Big Sur as a refuge for nonconformist, creative individuals seeking personal liberation.

But arriving at this state of symbiotic interaction with nature was not automatic. In fact it took years to break the habits of cultural conditioning and the expectations of society. The story of how Carolyn Kleefeld arrived in Big Sur and came to make the art that she does is a fascinating tale filled with larger-than-life figures and curious turns of events on an unlikely and unexpected voyage of life.

Carolyn Kleefeld was born in Catford, a section of London, England. She was the youngest child of Mark and Amelia Taper. The couple had two other children—Barry, the oldest, and Janice. The son of Polish émigrés to Great Britain, Mark Taper used perseverance and hard work to create a successful chain of London shoe stores. Astute investments in real estate allowed him to retire early. His wife, the former Amelia Lewis, was an artist who had done freelance illustrations for London's *Vogue*. She represented a more sensitive soul, a marked contrast to her business-minded husband. As Kleefeld later recalled, "I inherited two opposite tendencies: my mother's artistic temperament and my father's pioneering business acumen."[4] Later she would see balancing opposites as essential to her life's work.

When Mark Taper retired and left his business in England, he decided to move to California. To someone raised in the cold, damp climate of Britain, the sunshine of California offered an ideal lifestyle. The family settled first in Long Beach but after six months relocated to Santa Monica to be closer to the beach. Carolyn grew up attending Franklin Elementary School in Santa Monica and later the Westlake School for Girls. As the youngest child, she had a temperament that differed from others in the family. Her siblings were of a practical mind and eventually pursued paths in business. Carolyn preferred to read, draw, and retreat into the world of her imagination. She remembers staging for her mother's friends impromptu performances for which she would impersonate a host of imaginary characters.

Carolyn had a precocious talent, and at the age of nine she wrote and illustrated a book titled *The Nanose*. She remembers being inspired "by dust particles dancing in a sunbeam flooding my bedroom window." In her vivid imagination, each speck of dust was a tiny person, and she created a whole world for them to inhabit.

Mark and Amelia Taper with their children, Janice, Carolyn and Barry.

Page from Carolyn Taper,
The Nanose in Nanoseland, juvenilia,
Illustrated manuscript
11.75 x 9 inches

Carolyn Taper as a young ballerina.

As an adult reflecting back on this time, she realized there was a fascinating relationship behind her childhood imaginings and science, specifically with atoms and nanotechnology: "Through my impression of the dancing dust particles I had my first recorded interaction with atomic life. My art was the bridge, translating localized conception (dust particles) into atomic theory. I thus experienced intimate dialogue with the vaster universe."[5] This idea of the close relationship between the microcosmic and the macrocosmic would become a key component of her art and worldview.

Carolyn, the precocious writer, was also a great reader. She remembers that when she was around twelve years old, she discovered her first love in literature—Guy de Maupassant, the French 19th-century master of the short story. She also explored fantasy fiction and as a schoolgirl voraciously devoured books by Wolo, a pseudonym for Wolf Ehrhardt Anton Trutzschuler von Falkenstein. In the 1940s he wrote and illustrated five children's books based on mythic figures and imaginary realms. Wolo's stories gave the highly imaginative young girl a rich alternative to mundane reality. As an adult she continued to delight in creating fantasy images, not to escape from reality but to discover a heightened reality conducive to her active imagination.

She also found an outlet for her creativity and physical energy in horse-riding and dance, two art forms that allowed her to experience true existential freedom. She attended the Toland School of Ballet in Santa Monica from age five to age twelve. An opportunity arose to study at the Bolshoi Ballet in Moscow, but Amelia refused to let her daughter travel overseas at such a young age.[6]

Although bright and curious, Carolyn was too energetic and impatient to sit behind a desk and always felt stifled by formal schooling. She craved to be outdoors and to be free. Her first true love of her life was her horse, Mabel. More than a pet, Mabel was a great companion, and the two were inseparable. At a time when large areas of Los Angeles were still undeveloped, Carolyn would ride Mabel into the local canyons as well as from the Riviera Country Club to the Brentwood Country Club for tennis lessons. Together they won many trophies in riding competitions. Riding helped cement Carolyn's lifelong love for the outdoors, for animals, and for nature.[7]

Carolyn matured to be a winning athlete. Besides riding, she also played tennis. During her teen years, she rose to the rank of number one player in Santa Monica and Beverly Hills. Tennis was the requisite sport for young women from proper families, and Carolyn excelled. However, the family's move to Beverly Hills meant an overall change of lifestyle that did not suit her independent spirit. As Mark Taper's housing and banking businesses grew and prospered, he purchased a larger and more luxurious house. Carolyn did not fit in with the values of the new, more affluent neighborhood. To her, the emphasis on material goods and possessions felt shallow and superficial. As she later wrote,

> I was fifteen years old when my family decided to leave Santa Monica and move to Beverly Hills. Until then, the best part of my life had been riding my horse, Mabel, a kindred spirit, in the rural area surrounding my home.
>
> When we moved, this way of life was lost to the plastic and glitter of Beverly Hills. When friends visited, I was embarrassed by our house; some had never seen wall-to-wall carpeting in a bathroom. I felt uncomfortable because people tended to see the material world before the spiritual. When I was seen, it was as a business tycoon's daughter. No one saw into my soul. My family couldn't know me, nor could the society I inhabited.
>
> After I moved to Beverly Hills, I had Mabel put to sleep. She was old, wasn't well, wasn't eating, and therefore, I rationalized, couldn't survive going out to pasture. Although all of this was true, I see now that what I did to Mabel was what I was doing to myself, putting my own spirit to sleep along with hers. At school I separated from my unique friends and, instead, wanted to fit in with the exclusive club group.[8]

As the beautiful young daughter of a powerful and influential civic leader, Carolyn was expected to adhere to the expectations of her family and high society. In the postwar years Beverly Hills presented a world of conformity. Inhabited by the wealthy elite of Los Angeles, it was an enclave of financial achievement and material success. Carolyn sacrificed part of her spirit to fit into this world. She had the beauty, charm, and lively personality to succeed in this course, at least on the outside. For a time, she adopted the values of her new peer group and became popular on the nightclub scene. Through The Beverly Hills Tennis Club, she met and went to parties with Joe Pasternak, Richard Zanuck, Rock Hudson, Paul Newman, and Dinah Shore, among others. Her activities revolved around the most fascinating circles in Los Angeles at the time. She began to model and was represented by the Caroline Leonetti Agency.[9] She had an agent at the William Morris Agency and, after reading for some of the major studios, was offered a contract. Mark Taper exclaimed with pride that she was the first of his children to earn any money!

Carolyn married Travis Kleefeld, an actor and a singer who performed under the name of Tony Travis. He was a fixture of the Los Angeles club scene. Travis was handsome, talented, and charming—and Carolyn remembers having heard about him as an actor on the Perry Mason show. The couple became parents of two girls, Carla and Claudia. However, they divorced, and Carolyn focused on raising her children as a single mother.

The end of her marriage forced Carolyn Kleefeld to reevaluate her life. She decided it was time to leave Beverly Hills and in 1974 moved to Malibu. Seeking a quieter way of life, she rented a seaside bungalow on Malibu Road. The ocean became her backyard. Malibu at the time defined a casual bohemian lifestyle. Living at the beach, surrounded by air and water, the locals could leave the strict inhibitions of Los Angeles society behind. They were free to lead a life of their own making.

After graduating from Beverly Hills High School, she had attended Santa Monica City College, then she studied psychology, poetry, and painting for three years at UCLA. But the formal vigor of school was counter to her free spirit and inner creative needs. As she recalled,

> Not having the nature to be in the world, I have always been fatigued by public systems, schools and universities. I daydreamed and doodled my way through school, but was always fascinated by art and psychology. I found the subtler sensitivities of the natural world and its creatures more entrancing than academia. My spiritual survival was at stake no matter how comfortable my home. My imagination is my salvation; the world of ideas, my sport.[10]

While the narrow structures of a formal curriculum did not suit her independent spirit, in the 1970s she returned to school driven by a curiosity and a hunger for knowledge. She began taking courses in psychology through the UCLA Extension program. There she met an inspiring teacher, Dr. Carl Faber. He opened the doors to a new world of ideas. Kleefeld remembers him as being a "poet-shaman" and regards him as her "first mentor."

A psychologist and poet who taught at both UCLA and the Extension Program in the late 1960s and early 1970s, Carl Faber was a dynamic, caring, and brilliant professor who developed a devoted following. Because of his innovative attitude that addressed a wealth of serious issues from psychological and philosophical perspectives, his lectures routinely attracted audiences of several hundred. The originality of his broad-minded approach is seen in the title of a seminar—"Edges: On the Border of the Human Experience."

Faber's expansive, humanistic perspective on life was in attune with an immensely popular and influential cultural trend in the 1970s known as Humanistic Psychology. This movement was also known as Third Force Psychology because it represented an alternative to the narrow ideologies offered by Sigmund Freud's Psychoanalysis and B. F. Skinner's Behaviorism. Humanistic Psychology originated in the 1950s as an expansion upon the existential philosophies of Søren Kierkegaard and Jean-Paul Sartre. Rather than focusing on fragments of the personality, this new approach addressed the whole person as a dynamic, functioning organism. It also drew heavily upon Carl Jung, who advocated a holistic approach that emphasized "integration," a balance of contradictory forces within a self-actualized, healthy individual. Humanistic Psychology had a powerful impact on American culture because of its emphasis on uniquely human values and the fundamental issues of life, such as individuation, death, loneliness, freedom, and meaning.

In her own way, Kleefeld absorbed many of these ideals. She used the meditative environment of Malibu to embark on a new journey of the mind. A true autodidact, she began a self-directed program of intellectual discovery. As she later recounted,

> Yes, my first mentor was Dr. Carl Faber, then came the writings of Anaïs Nin. Other influences include: Herman Hesse, Rainer Maria Rilke, William Blake, Vincent van Gogh, Marc Chagall. Gustav Klimt, D.H. Lawrence, Baudelaire, Dylan Thomas, Benjamin de Casseres, Aldous Huxley, and Mozart. Then there is the powerful influence of my friends and contemporaries.[11]

This group of diverse writers, artists, and intellectuals were united in their radical independence and nonconformist views. Each was a freethinker who had the temerity to challenge the most cherished beliefs of their day. Kleefeld came to admire personal truth, boldness of thought, and visionary innovation as the highest of values.

Malibu served as the perfect home base for these self-directed intellectual explorations. During the 1970s, this community attracted a fascinating group of actors, musicians, and scientists—in general, creative types who were too independent in mind and spirit to fit in with conventional society. Malibu was rural and beautiful, providing access to the beach and nearby canyons. Since it was only ten miles from Los Angeles, it offered the ideal balance of a retreat from civilization that was still close to the big city. This idyllic community attracted an important group of free-spirited intellectuals. It was home to Kleefeld's good friend Dr. John C. Lilly. Lilly was a medical doctor, psychologist, and scientist who pioneered research into the intelligence of dolphins and invented the sensory deprivation tank. Another Malibu resident was Dr. Franz Janoff, the founder of Scream Therapy. Kleefeld was particularly close to actor Rod Steiger. She watched him teach Method Acting classes which reflected her own style of artistic expression, emphasizing that passionate creativity must draw upon real life experiences to create "artistic truth."

Some participants in *The Mavericks of the Mind* gathered at UCLA in 1994. *Clockwise from upper left:* Dr. Oscar Janiger, Laura Archera Huxley, Dr. John C. Lilly, Carolyn Kleefeld, Dr. Timothy Leary, and Nina Graboi.

Carolyn Kleefeld surrounded by lush vegetation in Hawaii.

Malibu in the 1970s served as a center for counterculture scientists, mystics, and intellectuals. These California renegades were at the forefront of a larger national trend that questioned the direction and values of conventional scientific "progress." In his 1975 book, *A Sense of the Cosmos*, Jacob Needleman noted that "the crisis of ecology, the threat of atomic war, and the disruption of the patterns of human life by advanced technology have all eroded what was once a general trust in the goodness of science."[12] Many thinkers at the time questioned the materialist base of Western physical science and looked for alternatives in the spiritual perspectives of Eastern religions and ancient philosophy.

Kleefeld thrived in this environment and was able to make the time to focus on her poetry. She met Anaïs Nin, a writer she had long admired, at the International Language Institute in West Los Angeles. They corresponded, and Nin encouraged the younger writer to "find your own voice." This guidance came at the right time, when Kleefeld had just begun her more contemplative life at the beach. At first she wrote poems simply for herself, but the response from people who read them convinced her to publish her work. Her first book of poetry, *Climates of the Mind*, came out in 1979. The title outlines a key theme in Kleefeld's worldview. The mind does not stand apart from nature but is a reflection of natural forces. As the body is subject to changing temperatures and climates, the imagination also generates its own environments and creates new worlds. Over the years, this publication would be followed by six additional books. In 1993 she was asked to participate in *Mavericks of the Mind: Conversations for the New Millennium* which gathered together interviews with individuals engaged in extending the boundaries of scientific thought. Her interview appeared alongside those of people such as John Lilly, Timothy Leary, Laura Huxley and Allen Ginsberg.[13]

It was shortly after she completed *Climates of the Mind* that Kleefeld visited Big Sur and joined a workshop at the Esalen Institute. Esalen was founded in 1962 by Michael Murphy and Richard Price, two psychologists who had studied together at Stanford University.[14] Murphy was the grandson of a couple who owned the hot springs in Big Sur and had tried unsuccessfully to develop it as a health spa. When Murphy and Price invited Alan Watts, a scholar and teacher of Zen Buddhism, to visit and offer lectures, a cultural phenomenon was born. By the fall of 1962 they were advertising weekend seminars in "The Human Potentialities," borrowing a phrase from Aldous Huxley who became a frequent visitor. The core ideology of Esalen focused on the belief that the human mind and spirit were capable of achieving vast wonders that lay largely untapped and unrealized. The name Esalen was chosen to honor the original inhabitants of the region—the Essellen Indians—and to capture the ideals of spirituality and insight derived from nature and from indigenous sources.

In Big Sur, Kleefeld discovered a place conducive to her creative sensibility as have countless others who have described their experiences as life-changing. Henry Miller, who lived in Big Sur between 1944 and 1962, wrote in his memoir, *Big Sur and the Oranges of Hieronymus Bosch*, that "Big Sur has a climate of its own and a character all its own. It is a region where extremes meet, a region where one is always conscious of weather, of space, of grandeur, and of eloquent silence."[15] This extraordinarily powerful place provides an invigorating and bracing exposure to nature and reality as an immediate experience. For Kleefeld this retreat from the modern world was the perfect place for a poet to mature and a visual artist to be born.

In 1980 Kleefeld purchased her home on a secluded point high above the waves. The house itself is modest and unassuming, yet it offers spectacular views. The sea appears as a breathtaking image that both surrounds the observer and also seems distant, extending toward infinity. Despite the vast physical dimensions, the ocean makes its presence known as an immediate, vital force. Big Sur is picturesque and seems benign, yet it bears the full brunt of powerful winter storms. In addition, Kleefeld's cliff top is subject to howling winds year-round which buffet the house, an ever-present reminder of the brute force of nature.

Carolyn Kleefeld painting outside her home in Big Sur.

She explained that her home in Big Sur is "a unique place to be."

> It has accelerated my internal journey, and simultaneously my art, to be in a place where I can create the space and time to let all that's possible happen. It's an enigmatic and challenging environment. It's been essential for me to be in the constant inspiration of nature, where I can be in a position to live my own natural rhythms, and define my own nature. Previously, I didn't have the time to do so. Here I'm able to create a world where I can live in my imagination as much of the time as possible.

> This wilderness is a place that allows me to be in a receptive and vulnerable state of being. Because I'm not dealing with the daily traffic of a city, I'm not having to use the defense mechanisms that dull my sensibilities. My sensitivities and sensibilities have the freedom to play, experiment and just be. Big Sur is a mirror for a beautiful state of mind, hence the real importance of keeping it unpolluted can't be stressed too much, since we have so few places left that can mirror the human soul.[16]

Henry Miller also noted that the seclusion and simplicity of Big Sur made it conducive for artists and for those who wanted to live a generative artistic life. He found that it had attracted people who had first experienced the world and then chosen to turn their backs on civilization,

> Starting anew, for this type, means leading a vagrant's life, tackling anything, clinging to nothing, reducing one's needs and desires, and eventually—out of a wisdom born of desperation—leading the life of an artist. Not, however, the type of artist we are familiar with. An artist, rather, whose sole interest is in creating, an artist who is indifferent to reward, fame, success.[17]

Kleefeld found such an artist in Edmund Kara (1925–2001), a sculptor and neighbor who became a close friend, muse, and inspiration. Kara had enjoyed a successful career working as an interior decorator and fashion designer, creating dresses for the likes of Lena Horne and Peggy Lee. But he tired of that world and in 1962 moved to Big Sur where he settled into a simple cabin beneath Kleefeld's house. There he lived a Spartan, monastic life. Requiring little in terms of personal comforts, he focused on his art, creating magnificent wood carvings. Today, his oak sculpture *Phoenix Bird* stands as a centerpiece of Nepenthe Restaurant, an internationally known landmark. Kleefeld looked upon Kara as a powerful influence. She recalled that his example confirmed her own attraction to living a simple, unassuming life, stripped of burdensome belongings.

When Kleefeld turned to making visual art as a passionate endeavor in 1983, she had no designs on the art world. In fact she paints from herself and for herself. This innocence and purity of approach places her in the category of Outsider Artist. These artists are distinguished by a lack of guile. They make art solely for themselves out of a deep-seated need to express something that cannot be conveyed in other means. Making art provides a way for Kleefeld to exercise her creative faculties. The resulting images, in turn, offer her a vision of her own psyche and the unknown.

The Humanistic Psychologists celebrated creativity. Although previously it was looked upon as a diversion, creativity was seized upon by a new generation of thinkers as a vital, constructive activity, essential to human existence. Books such as Arthur Koestler's *The Creative Act* of 1962 and Rollo May's *The Courage to Create* of 1975 set forth the belief that for individuals to realize their full potential, they had to stop repeating established truths and embark on a course of original self-discovery. Creativity in this sense is a sign of the individual's ability to address new situations and solve new problems. It offers a fresh and vital perspective. As Kleefeld noted, "Most artists are like engineers reproducing the familiar."[18] She maintains that "when artists are working directly from their emerging consciousness, their art is their most honest mirror."

True creativity involves breaking through inhibitions. In our society, which emphasizes market values and objectivity, attaining true creative freedom is fraught with challenges. To help overcome these obstacles, Kleefeld prefers to paint quickly, capturing the spontaneity of the moment. Working at this pace allows the hand to move more quickly than the mind. It allows the self to relinquish total control so that images can emerge spontaneously from deep within.

Working in the immediate moment involves chance. Kleefeld believes in spontaneity as a means to tap into truths that lay beyond oneself. In this, she belongs to a lineage of avant-garde artists such as the composer John Cage, who advocated using chance to undermine the role of ego in art. Indeterminate techniques create a situation of active non-intention. Kleefeld believes that when people let go and relinquish total control, they are in a better position to grasp the subtle messages and deep truths both within and around them.

Color is essential to the way Kleefeld works. Often a painting originates with a color impression—red, blue, or gold—that ignites her imagination and provides a starting point for a series of cascading relationships, synthesizing lyrics, color and poetic symbolism into unrestrained, liberating improvisations. As she explains, "Color holds emotional vibrations and emotions are the brain of the instincts." Through an honest instinctual response, we can grasp the full emotional dimensions of color. Kleefeld shares Kandinsky's analogy between color and music, where he described individual colors as notes on a key board. This synergistic mingling of visual and auditory senses also has deep meaning for Kleefeld, whose first passion in the arts was for ballet. To her, dance is music, music is poetry and poetry is painting. All senses and emotions mirror each other.

Kleefeld combined her art, poetry and prose in her 1998 book *The Alchemy of Possibility: Reinventing Your Personal Mythology*. This text has been described variously as a collection of "psychological insights" and as "an inspiring odyssey of the imagination." Culled from ten years of her journals, it reflects wisdom gained through experience. It was inspired by the *I Ching*, the ancient Chinese text that uses a symbol system to locate a hidden order within chance events. Its tenets emphasize the need to balance opposites, to understand life as a process, and to accept the inevitability of change. These beliefs are the very heart of Kleefeld's aesthetic and worldview. The artist wants to reach out to people who are isolated, so when *Climates of the Mind* was translated into Braille, a wish was realized. When her other books were also used in classes in psychology, creative writing and human potential, her dream was further fulfilled.

Carolyn Kleefeld once remarked that her approach to art was nicely summed up in a passage by the American author Benjamin de Casseres. In his book *Forty Immortals* of 1926, he produced a personal, passionate, and partisan account of a group of thinkers who revolutionized the world. His list began with Nietzsche and included philosophers such as Emerson and Spinoza; writers such as Shakespeare, Poe, and Strindberg; and poets such as William Blake, Baudelaire, and Walt Whitman. Kleefeld found a section in his description of Marinetti and Italian Futurism to be particularly apt:

> In painting they are prying behind the phenomenal. They give us the hieroglyphics of emotions and sensation. They not only substitute feeling for sight but they substitute themselves for nature. They evoke the other side of images, the reverse of the inspired dream. It is the very mysticism of realism or the realism of mysticism.[19]

Kleefeld also looks beyond appearance to find the essence within. By remaining receptive to subtle forces, she is able to capture and reflect truths about the nature of the universe that most people seem to miss. The phrase "reverse of the inspired dream" is important in understanding Kleefeld's art, for she is not interested in projecting her dreams or her ego. The opposite is true. She sees herself more as a passive receiver. Some may look upon her art as a form of mysticism, but Kleefeld has no interest in the arcane and the occult.

Rather she understands the entire world as a great metaphysical structure involving the essential mysteries of time, space, matter, and fate. She paints to reveal these eternally mysterious truths. By capturing these universal wonders in a work of art, she invites us to grasp the essential paradox of life. That is the great gift of her art.

1   "Singing Songs of Ecstasy with Carolyn Mary Kleefeld," in David Jay Brown and Rebecca McClen Novick, *Mavericks of the Mind: Conversations for the New Millennium* (Freedom, CA: The Crossing Press, 1993), 161.

2   Paul Klee quoted in Jonathon Williams, "Eyes Outside and Eyes Inside," in Maurice Tuchman and Carol S. Eliel, *Parallel Visions: Modern Artists and Outsider Art* (Los Angeles County Museum of Art/Princeton, NJ: Princeton University Press, 1992), 15.

3   *Mavericks of the Mind*, 162.

4   Carolyn Mary Kleefeld, *The Alchemy of Possibility* (Carmel, CA: Merrill-West Publishing, 1998), 224.

5   *Mavericks of the Mind*, 159.

6   The Toland School held recitals at the Wadsworth Theater in Los Angeles. Decades later, in 1997, Kleefeld spoke on the same stage at a memorial to her friend, the Beat poet Allen Ginsberg. This is only one instance of the moments of synergy, of wondrous coincidence or fortuitous parallels, that she would explore throughout her life.

7   In another synergistic coincidence, when Carolyn was 12 she met Jane Fonda while riding Mabel in Mandeville Canyon. Decades later they became neighbors when Jane was married to Ted Turner, who had purchased a home next to Carolyn's in Big Sur.

8   Kleefeld, *Alchemy of Possibility*, 177.

9   Caroline Leonetti was an actress who later married financier Howard F. Ahmanson.

10 Kleefeld, *Alchemy of Possibility*, 178.

11 *Mavericks of the Mind*, 161.

12 Jacob Needleman, *A Sense of the Cosmos: The Encounter of Modern Science and Ancient Truth* (New York: Doubleday, 1975), 1.

13 *Mavericks of the Mind* proposed to explore a paradigm shift in understanding human consciousness at the dawn of the 21st century.

14 For a history of Esalen see Jeffrey J. Kripal, *Esalen: America and the Religion of No Religion* (Chicago: University of Chicago Press, 2007)

15 Henry Miller, *Big Sur and the Oranges of Hieronymus Bosch* (New York: New Directions, 1957), 4.

16 *Mavericks of the Mind*, 159.

17 Henry Miller, *Big Sur*, 17.

18 *Mavericks of the Mind*, 160.

19 Benjamin de Casseres, *Forty Immortals* (New York: Seven Arts Publishing Company, 1926), 252.

Artist Statement

Art, like music, offers a language beyond words. To be innovative, it must be created from an inner wilderness, free of stale and redundant concepts.

If art arises from an inner necessity to express rather than from a preconceived idea of beauty or style, then it can reflect, in symbolic imagery, our primal nature and oneness with all things.

Through the instrument of my being, I let intuitive experiment choose color and form, a practice of invention comparable to musical improvisation.

For me art is a spontaneous journey on the crest of the Tao's wave, an exploration born of passion, spawned by the Mystery. Initially, I am the maiden falling in love—then later, the ruthless editor-analyst.

Ultimately art is an innocent interactive mirror of my innermost process, whisking me out of time into the Timeless. My life's passion is to create art from this unconditioned well of being and to inspire such a journey in others.

Books by Carolyn Mary Kleefeld

Climates of the Mind (Los Angeles: The Horse and Bird Press, 1979).

Satan Sleeps with the Holy: Word Paintings (Los Angeles: The Horse and Bird Press, 1982).

Lovers in Evolution (Los Angeles: The Horse and Bird Press, 1983).

Songs of Ecstasy (Los Angeles: Gallerie Illuminati, 1990).

The Alchemy of Possibility: Reinventing Your Personal Mythology (Carmel: Merrill-West Publishing, 1998).

Kissing Darkness: Love Poems and Art (Ashland, Oregon: RiverWood Books, 2003), with David Wayne Dunn.

Soul Seeds: Revelations and Drawings (Merrick, NY: Cross-Cultural Communications, 2008).

Interview in David Jay Brown and Rebecca McClen Novick, *Mavericks of the Mind: Conversations for the New Millennium* (Freedom, CA: The Crossing Press, 1993).

The artist's personal website can be found at: http://carolynmarykleefeld.com/.

Carolyn Kleefeld working on one of her *Cosmic Abstractions*.

Cleo
1984
Watercolor on paper
14 x 12 inches

Early Works

Once Kleefeld was settled in Big Sur she focused on her visual art. She had always shown a fascination with drawing, as evinced by her youthful *Nanose,* and had studied art at UCLA. But she embarked on painting with a new sense of seriousness and purpose. The media she chose to work with were primarily water media— various combinations of watercolor, metallics, ink, and acrylic on paper and museum board. These materials were close to a writer's tools and being fluid, helped to expand her poetry into visual art.

One of her first works was *Cleo* (1984), a watercolor on paper. This painting depicts an adult woman and can be thought of as a self-portrait. But portrait is not exactly the best term. Features are generalized to the point where it would be difficult to recognize the person represented. Female "presence" might be more accurate for presence is perhaps the most powerful quality of this small but intense and deeply symbolic painting. The head asserts itself with certainty despite being indistinct and largely formless. It looms above the vague form of shoulders, creating a disembodied effect. Within this mysterious face, the eyes are the most prominent feature. Dark pupils radiate with a resolve that conveys both sight and insight.

Cleo conveys a force that belies its modest dimensions. If one where to ascribe an art historical label to this image, it would be called Symbolist. Symbolism was a dominant current in late nineteenth century art. Symbolist artists, such as Paul Gauguin and Gustav Moreau, sought a single concentrated image that would carry a potent and resonant meaning that extended far beyond the physical limits of the picture. One recurring theme in Symbolist art was the disembodied head. By detaching the head from the body, artists were able to concentrate attention on all that we associate with the mind. It symbolized the vast and mystifying world of mental activity, hinting at the wondrous capacity of the brain to dream, reflect, remember, think, and imagine.

Kleefeld's *Cleo* bears a striking resemblance to some of the self-portraits created by modernist composer Arnold Schoenberg. He turned to painting in 1907, at the age of 33, when his experiments with nontonal composition brought him public rejection and ridicule. His life and music in crisis, he turned to painting as a bold attempt to reassert his self and his creative identity. Like *Cleo,* his self-portraits are strictly frontal and symmetrical, with the eyes focused directly ahead. In the more abstract versions, he abandoned attempts to capture his likeness and emphasized the gaze of his staring eyes. They burn with the intensity of a seer. No longer fixated on the external world, they perceive a deeper truth and a larger vision. It is fitting that Kleefeld would evoke a similar form at a similar point in her life, a time of beginning, transition and reaffirmation.

Because it is so frontal and centered, *Cleo* also alludes to religious icons and to images of the Holy Face. In Catholicism, the practice of revering the face of Christ derives from a representation of His face, miraculously transferred to the veil of Veronica, a woman who tended to Him during His Passion. It was this work of art—produced not by human hands but from Christ's very body—that helped generate the medieval icon tradition. Icons were more than simple representations of religious figures. They were thought to embody the presence and spirit of the person depicted. Through the sheer intensity of the image, *Cleo* also conveys the aura of a living being, of a soul beyond physical body.

The Tree Face of Metamorphosis
1986
Mixed media on paper canvas
24 x 18 inches

The Asparagus Lady
1985
Mixed media on board
27.75 x 21.75 inches

This image also resembles a mask. It does not look like the artist and can be thought of as a persona. The term "persona" implies an identity or role that someone assumes. The word derives from the term for the classical actor of the ancient world. Psychologist Carl Jung wrote that "the persona is a semblance, a two-dimensional reality."[1] It is a fictional construct we adopt to better cope with reality. The mask-like quality of *Cleo* reminds us that our self is always self-constructed. Kleefeld was investigating her own identity and created this image as part of a process of self-exploration. She depicts herself as focused and resolute but also fragile and vulnerable. It is worth noting that in Greek mythology Cleo was the muse of history. As a living presence that exists before us in real time and space, it reminds us that history is something to be made, not merely remembered.

The motif of the floating head was a prevalent theme in Kleefeld's art at this time and reappears in *Tree Face of Metamorphosis* (1986). Instead of a mottled, indistinct background, this figure is surrounded by an abstract texture that appears floral or vegetal. *Tree Face* is a living thing, but its world is more arboreal than human.

Tree Face belongs to a long history of depictions of the Green Man, a woodland deity believed to dwell in northern forests of medieval Europe. In art this creature was depicted as human but wore a dense growth of branches and leaves. Considered to be a guardian of nature, he had the power to bring rain to nourish fields and livestock. Although the Green Man was a pagan deity, he was so essential to the life of a community that Christian churches often included representations of him within the foliate capitals of Gothic cathedrals.

Like the pagans who celebrated the original Green Man, Kleefeld recognizes the importance of respecting the spirit of nature and living in harmony with the natural world. While the modern world tries to triumph over nature, denying its rhythms and processes, she feels that we must return to our roots, which includes a sense of our essential rootedness within nature. Moving to Big Sur, and embracing nature's order, with all its breathtaking beauty and unpredictable terror, was a statement of her deep personal convictions. She was searching for origins, both in nature's deep structure and in her own ancestry. Like many of her paintings, *Tree Face of Metamorphosis* can be seen as a surrogate self-portrait, an image of a spiritual searcher who has chosen to lead a more natural path in life.

The dynamic presence seen in *Cleo* takes a new form and assumes a new direction in *Un-Dryad* (1986). Although the face is similar, it now has a body that glimmers in vibrant emerald greens. In Greek mythology, dryads were tree nymphs, or female spirits of nature. The word derives from the Greek word for "oak" and these spirits were closely associated with that species of tree. Although long-lived, dryads were mortal and fated to die. These shy and retiring creatures were often bound to a specific locality and within Greek culture often symbolized marriageable young women.

Kleefeld's *Un-Dryad* is the opposite of the figures in Greek myths. This being is a bold extrovert with arms wildly outstretched like the wings of a bird. Whereas nymphs were subordinate to the true deities, *Un-Dryad* proudly proclaims its independence and has no superiors. It is ruled only by a lively and wondrously unruly spirit. The word "spirit" derives from the Latin "spiritus," which means "breath" but also "soul, courage, and vigor." *Un-Dryad* declares its own presence with a vigorous courage.

In *Asparagus Lady* (1985) Kleefeld continues to explore analogies between the human and vegetable worlds. Asparagus is one of the most fascinating plants because of its curious relationship to time. It is one of the slowest growing of vegetables, often taking years for a bed to establish itself. Yet once the plant has matured, it will send up large shoots virtually overnight. The speed with which they emerge and grow seems magical. Kleefeld saw in asparagus a symbol of her own growth as an artist. By the time she made *Asparagus Lady*, she was painting quickly, spontaneously, and was prolific, producing up to forty paintings a month.

Un-Dryad
1986
Acrylic on board
40 x 32 inches

Paradisiacal Creatures
1986
Mixed media on board
30 x 40 inches

La Dance
1986
Acrylic on board
30 x 24 inches

These early works focus on female figures and all can be thought of as symbolic self-portraits. Kleefeld created these works in a process of organic unfolding. They allowed her to externalize and explore her own states of mind. Although all emanating from deep within her consciousness, each image is unique. Variations reveal different facets of her personality. Carl Jung referred to this process of emerging uniqueness as individuation. In general this term refers to the ways an individual organism becomes separate and distinct from others. Jung saw this open-ended process of psychological maturation as essential to mental well-being. In these surrogate self-portraits, Kleefeld provides a model of how individuals can peer deep inside to explore and understand one's true nature. She sees them, in her own words, "as interactive mirrors." They are revelatory images that project but also reflect.

Individuation involves more than just the self for humans are social creatures. We learn and grow through our interactions with others. As her art progressed, Kleefeld began to explore groupings of figures. One important theme centered on couples. In *La Dance* (1986), two creatures undulate in parallel movements. They have long tapering necks and sinuous bodies and resemble either wading birds or snakes. Snakes are often feared in western culture. It was the snake that coaxed Eve to defy God's law and eat from the Tree of Life. But in ancient and non-western cultures, the snake often carries more positive meanings. Because snakes shed their skin and emerge renewed, they are often looked upon as symbols of regeneration and rebirth.

Although their movements mimic one another, the figures stand apart and are differentiated through color. The dark blue form feels masculine and the pink one feminine. Their dance is a ballet of closeness and detachment, mimicking the ebb and flow of real human relationships. Dancing is not simply a frivolous pastime. In his pioneering study on religion and art, *Sacred and Profane Beauty*, professor Gerardus van der Leeuw wrote: "The dance is neither an 'art' in a present-day, one-sided aesthetic sense, nor an entertainment. It is half ritual, half-work, and both together."[2] He traced the origin of dance to primitive peoples who made no distinction between "prayer, work, and dance."

In *La Dance*, Kleefeld's figures move with a formal rhythm that recalls this sense of primal ritual. The curves of their bodies are regular and symmetrical. They flow in tandem, mirroring each other's movements as a type of call-and-response. Because the curving movements are so ceremonial, they convey a sense of conscious purpose. Modern people all dance, each and every day. But the dance-like quality of our daily movements has been repressed by centuries of regimented labor. The practical demands of the office, factory, and store hinder our natural impulse. This painting can be seen as a celebration of instincts that we have suppressed for too long. Kleefeld danced in her youth and this painting expresses a continuation of that original passion. It is a plea for individuals to find the natural rhythms that lie deep within all of us.

In *Paradisiacal Creatures* (1986) the pair of animals clearly represents birds. In comparison with *La Dance*, these creatures are larger, full-bodied, and more robust. Their beaks touch in a loving gesture, and they are proudly intimate, with a more mature sense of commitment. The crests resemble crowns, giving them a regal aura. They seem like the king and queen of a magical realm, perhaps people who have been transformed into birds. For Kleefeld, these are not just animals but bird-like fantasy creatures; they function as archetypal symbols.

Carl Jung developed the concept of archetypes to convey his belief that the human mind is predisposed to certain great themes and events that play an essential role in the development of human life. These powerful and universal symbols include archetypal events such as birth, death, initiation, marriage, as well as archetypal figures such as mother, father, child, deity, hero, etc. Jung believed that every human is born with these concepts ingrained in our psyche. The bird can be thought of as an archetypal image. It is a cross-cultural, timeless symbol of flight and freedom. The Surrealist artist Max Ernst was so enthralled by birds that he adopted a bird-like alter-ego named "Loplop" and claimed that he arrived on Earth when he was hatched from an egg.[3] *Paradisiacal Creatures* conveys the Surrealist ideal of a fanciful realm more wondrous than our waking reality.

Kleefeld's serious forays into painting are autobiographical. More importantly, they are also diaristic. They record her thinking and being on that particular day. Diaries are a vital source of specific and detailed information about the human condition. Henry Miller was one who grasped the importance of this art form to the modern world. In discussing the diaries of his friend and one-time lover, Anaïs Nin, Miller wrote,

> The chief concern of the diarist is not with truth, though it may seem to be, any more than the chief concern of the conscious artist is with beauty. Beauty and truth are the by-products in a quest for something beyond either of these. But just as we are impressed by the beauty of a work of art, so we are impressed by the truth and sincerity of a diary. We have the illusion, in reading the pages of an intimate journal, that we are face to face with the soul of its author.[4]

Miller appreciated the fact that in a society of increasing conformity, it becomes a brave act of singular courage to look closely at oneself and honestly relay what one sees. Kleefeld's paintings take such a bold stance. They expose the face of their author with a disarming candor.

---

1 Carl G. Jung, *The Basic Writings*, trans. and ed. Violet Staub de Laszlo (New York: Modern Library, 1959), 138.

2 Gerardus van der Leeuw, *Sacred and Profane Beauty: The Holy in Art* (New York: Abingdon Press, 1963), 16.

3 Charlotte Stokes, "Surrealist Persona: Max Ernst's "Loplop, Superior of Birds," *Simiolus: Netherlands Quarterly for the History of Art*, 13, no. 3/4 (1983), 225-234.

4 Henry Miller, "Un Etre Etoilique," in Lawrence Durrell, ed., *The Henry Miller Reader* (New York: New Directions, 1959), 289.

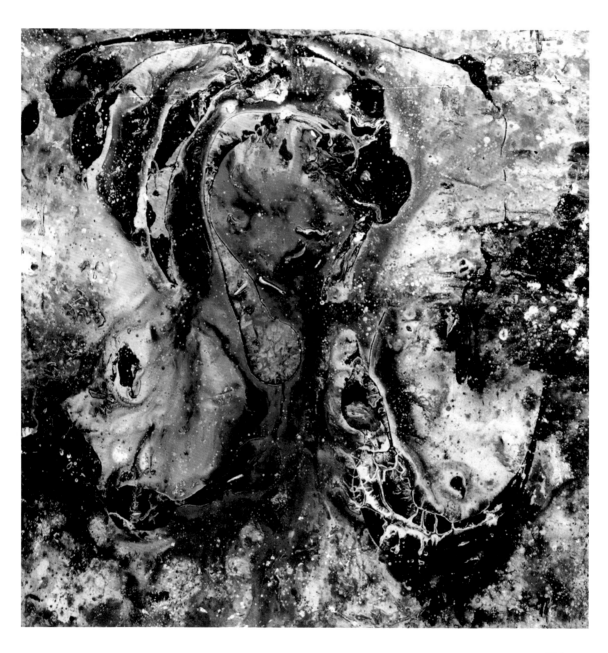

Alchemy
1991
Acrylic and gouache on canvas
48 x 48 inches

Cosmic Abstractions

Around 1986—87, Kleefeld embarked on a new series of work she later called her *Cosmic Abstractions*. These paintings were much larger than her first efforts and involved a more expansive sense of both the artist's place in the world and her function as a creator. Many of these paintings constitute the largest she has ever made. She pushed scale from inches to feet and switched media from paper to board and canvas. These changes reflected an important growth of self-image. No longer a writer who painted, she now saw herself as a poet *and* a painter. The two activities became equal outlets for her creative ideas. She also changed her working methods, and instead of painting on a table or easel, she took the intuitive step of placing her canvas on the floor. She painted by standing above and upon her canvas. This practice of pouring fluid paint from above was pioneered by Jackson Pollock, but in Kleefeld's hands the technique represented a new and varied range of possibilities that expanded her work into a more universal perspective.

An important early *Cosmic Abstraction* is *I Stomp Down Brush* (1986). Measuring almost four by six feet, it was painted on board. She placed a panel on the floor and dripped and splattered paint onto the surface. The method allowed her to explore the physical scope of her materials, learning how to use them to literally widen her own reach as an artist. As she covered her board with patterns of paint, she felt she recognized an image emerging in the center. It was an abstract personage, much like those in her earlier paintings, but now it was a full figure standing tall and erect. The stance of this creature mirrored that of the artist as she stood upright, working on the painting.

The title offers an important key. People stomp down brush in order to clear overgrown areas. This act of crushing unwanted vegetation is practical, primal, and primitive . But Kleefeld was not thinking of horticulture when she made this work. She wanted to stomp down the brush of her mind. To her, it was a metaphor for removing the unwanted debris of her psyche and for destructuring decades of conditioning. She shed old mental habits and reconditioned herself to be open to the multidimensional. Stomping is a crude but basic form of movement. Gerardus van der Leeuw believed that the stomp became the beginning of the dance which eventually led to the birth of all the arts.[1] Stomping down brush is a simple but dance-like and mysterious act of destruction and creation.

The painting conveys the raw primitive energy of the subject. The dripped white lines and splatters resemble the broken ends of cracked, dry brush. But they also allude to sparks of magical light. In creating this work, Kleefeld came to see her art as affecting a type of magical transformation. The alter-ego figure stands like a magician, proud of its ability to conjure its environment and world. The act of painting paralleled the act of stomping down brush. Both allowed her to realize new dimensions.

Winged Creation (1987) was painted only one year later, but demonstrates a greater command of her materials and techniques. Upon a richly glowing red ground, two birds emerge from a field of primordial chaos. They are stately, royal and seem untroubled by the anarchy around them. In fact, they seem to emerge from it, drawing sustenance from the disorder. These birds can be seen as representing the ancient Phoenix, the mythic bird that renews itself from destruction.

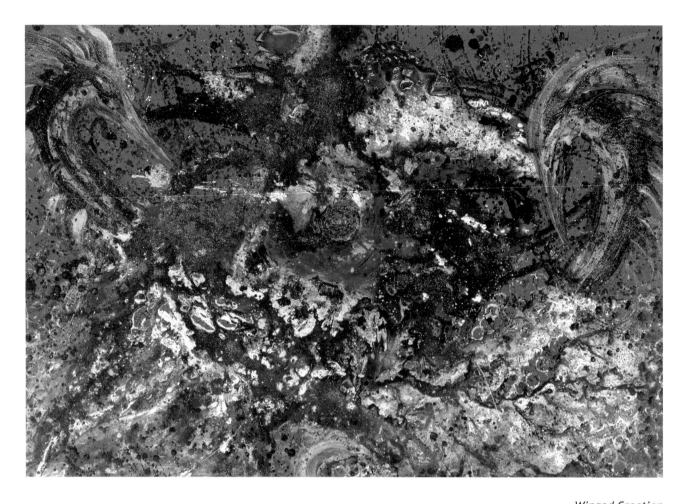

Winged Creation
1987
Mixed media on board
40 x 60 inches

I Stomp Down Brush
1986
Mixed media on canvas
40 x 72 inches

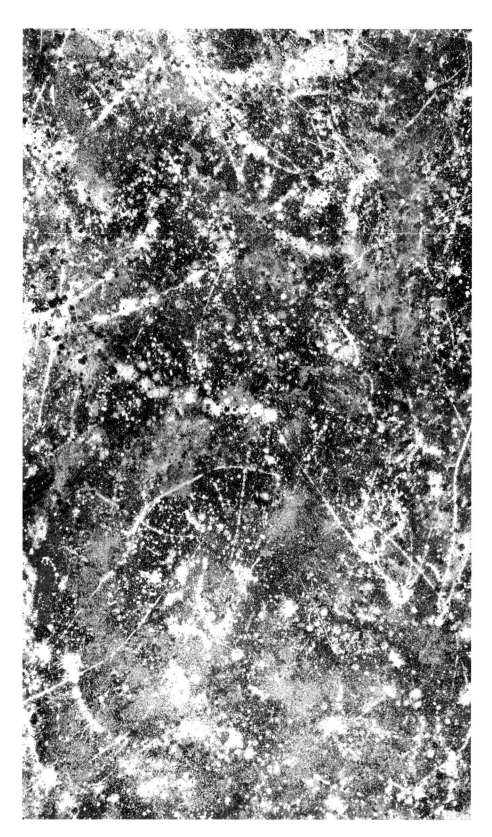

Galactic Vision
1988
Mixed media on canvas
80 x 48 inches

These creatures face one another in a powerful pairing. Art historians refer to this organizing logic as bilateral symmetry. This method of pictorial composition is ancient and features two objects that face each other in a mirror image. Bilateral symmetry first arose and was common in the art of the Iron and Bronze Ages, at the dawn of civilization. These early examples often depicted figures of great violent force, such as warriors or wild animals. Bilateral symmetry became an effective way of representing fierce primal power and keeping it under artistic control.

In *Galactic Vision* (1988) Kleefeld created a work that best conveys two key ideas embodied in all her *Cosmic Abstractions*: the drip painting (art) and the cosmos (nature). This work probably comes closest to resembling classic poured paintings by Jackson Pollock, and in this proximity we are able to discern vital affinities and differences. Pollock revolutionized painting in 1948 when he took the canvas off the easel, placed it on the floor of his studio, and worked by applying fluid paint from above. He altered all previous ideas of composition by rejecting part-to-part relationships in order to create the first "all-over" paintings. Film footage of him painting reveals a man operating with the intensely graceful moves of an animal. He painted in a rhythmic dance, using gesture to record the slightest tremors of his consciousness. As a result, his dripped and poured line became a seismograph of his psychological being. He saw art as an assertive projection of his psyche. When Pollock proudly declared, "I am Nature," he boldly revealed his belief in the force and supremacy of his ego.

While Kleefeld's *Galactic Vision* may look like a Pollock painting on the surface, this resemblance is superficial. Her purpose and intent are the opposite of his. She celebrates the wonders and mysteries of nature; she does not declare her own personality. She sees everyday life as an inseparable part of that larger wondrous realm we call the universe. Part of her effort to understand her own life means coming to grips with the mysteries of creation. The material of paint functions as a metaphor for matter in the universe. Both adhere to the same laws of physics and reveal the same cosmic truths. Accidents on canvas reflect chance and fate as existential principles. The painting functions as a microcosm of the greater macrocosm that is life itself.

Her title for this series, *Cosmic Abstractions,* is filled with rich cultural implications. The word "cosmos" possesses a special resonance that has captivated the minds of thinkers and artists throughout time. For the ancient Greeks, the word "cosmos" was the opposite of "chaos" and signified a harmonious system, implying a logical order behind all of creation. The rise of observational science in the Renaissance shattered medieval conceptions of a fixed universe and replaced them with a new appreciation of the cosmos as an array of natural bodies that move through space. When the Romantic movement arose in the early 19th century, many pondered the concept of the cosmos as being infinite. Introspective artists such as the German landscape painter Carl David Friedrich and the English poet William Blake looked into the sky and saw great religious truths. Kleefeld regards Blake as one of her favorite poets and continues this trend of Romantic reflection into the deep bond between religion and nature. In popular culture, the subject of the cosmos captured the hearts and minds of Americans with the broadcast of the PBS television series, *Cosmos: A Personal Voyage*, in 1980. Hosted by astronomer Carl Sagan, this series promoted the idea of the cosmos as a vast but harmonious realm, and became the most popular educational program on American television at the time.

Galactic Vision and similar works resemble the visual form of the cosmos. Spots and speckles of paints look like the array of stars and celestial bodies visible in the night sky. But on a deeper level, these paintings also reflect the same elemental forces that work to shape physical reality. Her gestural marks extended out from her arms but remained linked to the core of her body. The resulting structure reflects the powers of expansion and compression. Forms coalesce and open up, spreading and contracting with the same energy that gave form to the planets and stars. Drops of paint seem like cosmic dust—matter that seems insignificant in itself but is capable of shaping itself into greater wholes with enormous formative potential.

While Kleefeld's poured paintings mirror the molecular look of the cosmos they also reflect the luminous, unfolding nature of enlightened consciousness. This idea can be traced to an important book of 1901 titled *Cosmic Consciousness*. Written by Richard Maurice Bucke, a progressive 19th century Canadian psychologist who worked in the years just before Freud's breakthrough studies, this text sought to describe a particular mode of heightened human experience. Bucke was interested in those rare moments when individuals experience a feeling of transcendence—a simultaneous feeling of selflessness, expansiveness, and oneness with the universe. He cited accounts of these experiences within the lives of historical individuals ranging from religious figures, such as the Buddha and Jesus Christ; to poets such as Dante, William Blake and his friend, Walt Whitman; and to common citizens, including friends and neighbors. According to Bucke, these states of cosmic consciousness represented the highest state of the human mind and involved a feeling of light, wellness, and spiritual connectedness as well as a special sense that the universe itself was vibrating and radiant, both within and without.

Later psychologists further developed Bucke's early explorations into feelings of personal transcendence. The humanist psychologist Abraham Maslow described this phenomenon by introducing the term "peak experience." In his 1964 book, *Religions, Values, and Peak Experiences*, he identified certain moments marked by feelings of intense happiness and well-being, wonder and awe, which at times also involve an awareness of a transcendent higher truth. He believed that these experiences are often sparked by exposure to art, music, love, or nature. They tend to increase the individual's sense of determination, empathy, and creativity. Psychologist Mihály Csíkszentmihályi further explored these ideas beginning in the 1970s which led to his 1990 book, *Flow: The Psychology of Optimal Experience*. His research found that people in a state of flow discover themselves absorbed in activities of intense focus and engagement. They lose a sense of time and gain a feeling of comfort, well-being, and connectedness. Carolyn Kleefeld created her *Cosmic Abstractions* in such a state of flow. The paintings exemplify the value of allowing oneself the freedom to let go of inhibitions and accept the liberating joy of improvisation.

A sense of living radiance permeates paintings such as *Monarch Code*, *Uncorrupted Mystery* and *Voodoo Mountain Storm* (all 1990). They mark an advance in technique from *Galatic Vision*, which was painted with a sense of haphazard openness that mimics the irregular patterns of matter that coalesces by chance. By 1990 her mastery of her working procedure had matured significantly. With greater confidence and assurance of her means, she began to produce more complicated images with swirling rhythms and unfolding patterns. Whereas the earliest *Cosmic Abstractions* were governed by a sense of randomness, these new paintings reveal the beauty inherent in the concept of flow. They seem Baroque with their sheer richness and visual splendor. Like typical examples of Baroque art, they are about light and infinity.

Kleefeld painted these works by exploiting paint's capacity to move like a liquid. Working in various water-based media, ranging from acrylic to metallics and gouache to ink, she learned that by adding water or medium she could alter the texture of her paint from a thick paste to an easy moving fluid. She also discovered ways to gently direct the puddle of paint. By lifting portions of the loose canvas, by spraying water, or by creating depressions in select spots, she could direct the flow. Painting became a process of coaxing and guiding liquid color.

Water is famous for its curious and paradoxical physical properties. One may say it has its own intelligence, its own quirky way of behaving and interacting with other things. Because of the hydrogen bond, water molecules tend to stick to one another. This physical affinity allows water to move like a mass without assuming the stable form of a solid. Theodor Schwenk (1910-1986) was an eccentric, visionary scientist who pioneered research into the nature of water. One of his books, *Sensitive Chaos* of 1971, helped influence the development of Chaos theory.[2] He identified archetypal patterns, based on water's propensity to move in specific forms such as waves, vortices, spirals and winding paths. He believed that the mutability of water

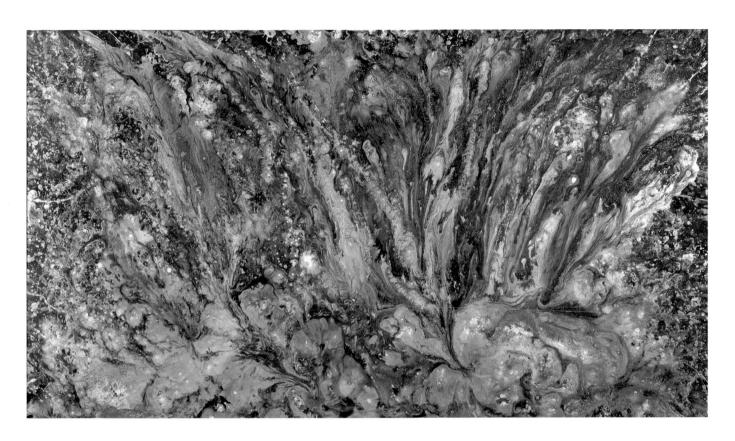

Uncorrupted Mystery
1990
Mixed media on canvas
40 x 72 inches

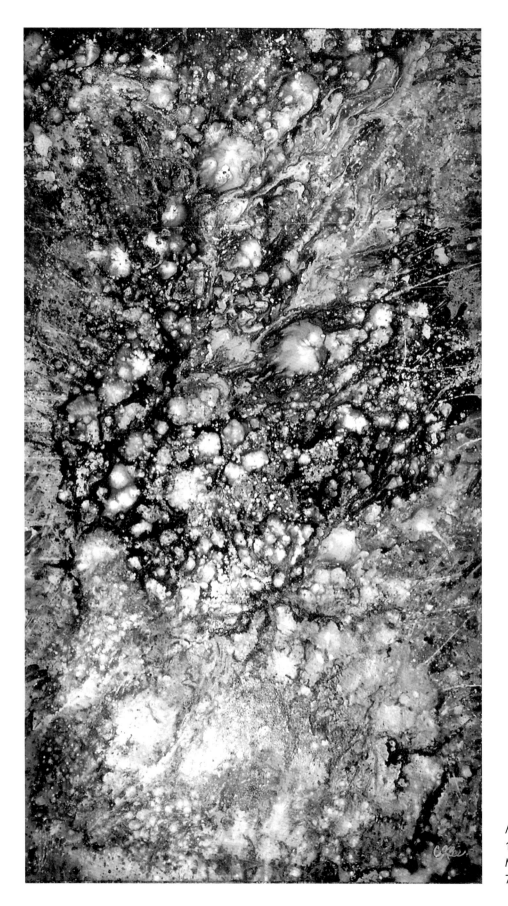

Monarch Code
1990
Mixed media on canvas
72 x 40 inches

served as a model for an ideal, fluid state of human consciousness. Although Kleefeld did not know or read the work of Schwenk, many of her *Cosmic Abstractions* explore the cyclical, swirling rhythms he identified.

These paintings, especially *Monarch Code* and *Uncorrupted Mystery*, radiate with an inner light. They glitter and glow—literally. In creating these mixed-media paintings, Kleefeld employed an array of art materials and used not only traditional paints but also metallic pigments. Metallic ink and paint, also known as "metal flake," use small pieces of metal to catch and reflect light to create sparkle. The gleam and twinkle of the surface is pretty and may seem merely decorative. But the choice and use of shiny material reflects deeper issues, ranging from the feminine to the transcendent to the psychological.

Attractive, glittering materials are often associated with the feminine. One is reminded of articles of women's fashion featuring lame and sequins. Artist Miriam Schapiro coined the word "femmage" in the 1970s in an attempt to assert the validity of patterns, textiles, and other decorative artforms that had traditionally been seen as minor arts. She introduced this term—an ingenious wedding of "feminine" and "collage"—in order to assert the importance of art that was unabashedly decorative and lavishly beautiful. Critic Donald Kuspit proposed another term, "Cosmic Transcendentalism," that he linked to the use of metallic substances in certain artists of the late 1970s. He perceived this interest in glimmering "surface-light" as alluding to traditional notions of the sublime.[3] Both these readings illuminate Kleefeld's use of these materials.

There is another dimension to Kleefeld's use of metallic colors that raises the issue of alchemy. In his book, *The Forge and the Crucible*, scholar of religion Mircea Eliade explored the deep connections between alchemy and metalworking.[4] He demonstrated that at the dawn of civilization, people began to work the raw iron found in meteorites. Gradually they learned to heat ore to extract metal, and in this process of transformation, alchemy was born.

Many people today dismiss alchemy as a misguided pseudo-science that was tainted by medieval ignorance and superstition. One person who saw great treasures in the discipline was Carl Jung. His research into the literature of the field indicated that the historic alchemists were concerned foremost not with changing matter but with transforming the mind. Alchemy was a process of bringing about a wondrous and mysterious transformation within the human soul. Jung found that many of the key concepts explored by Renaissance alchemists bore fascinating parallels to his own work in analytical psychology. He found the parallels between alchemy and modern psychology to be so compelling that he devoted the last years of his life to alchemical studies.

Kleefeld delved into psychology most fully in the 1970s. Her teachers and friends at the time included many Humanist Psychologists sympathetic to the work of Jung. She was particularly fascinated by Jung's ideas of alchemy as a psychological process. When she wrote a book in 1998 containing philosophical reflections on life she chose the title, *The Alchemy of Possibility*. The *Cosmic Abstractions* embody an important feature of alchemical thinking. The alchemists practiced a kind of meditation similar to Jung's technique of active imagination. By freely contemplating images that arise spontaneously in one's life, one is able to dialogue with the archetypal elements within the unconscious. This best describes Kleefeld's process of painting. Alchemical reflection is what allows her to create and develop a whole body of probing, provocative, and fertile images.

In *Alchemy* (1991) she honors the process of psychological growth. Jung believed that in order to be a fully realized and healthy individual one has to embrace the darker or negative sides of the personality, which he called the Shadow. Only by accepting what is dark, can one transcend it and attain a higher state of consciousness. *Alchemy* consists of pink (feminine) and black (shadow) shapes that swirl together in muscular conflict. From this sea of turmoil, a solid pink mass emerges in the center. It looks like a torso and could represent the artist herself. This strong, solid body arises triumphantly from the surrounding chaos as a statement of inner strength. In this painting Kleefeld creates a testament to the pioneering work in psychology and alchemy of Carl Jung

In a related work, *Atoms Mirror Atoms* (1991), Kleefeld creates a centralized mass with petals or tendrils that radiate outward. It reflects her belief that nothing occurs in isolation. As she explains, this phrase "expresses a poetic synthesis of some key principles of religion and physics: Every action has an equal and opposite reaction; What you sow so shall you reap; Like not only attracts, but begets like."[5] When Kleefeld speaks of atoms she is not referring to just the building blocks of matter postulated by science. She uses the word to refer to a host of things that are small and dear yet are essential and reflect a greater reality. As in the *Nanose* of her childhood, Kleefeld always had a predilection to see entire worlds within a speck of dust. She possessed the same romantic, poetic sensibility of a poet-artist like William Blake who wrote: "To see a World in a Grain of Sand/And a Heaven in a Wild Flower,/Hold Infinity in the palm of your hand/And Eternity in an hour."[6]

In *The Egyptian Space Goddess* (1990) and *Friendly Aliens* (1990), figures seem to emerge magically from the void. The being in *The Egyptian Space Goddess* is grand and glorious. A luminous creature with boldly outstretched arms, it sweeps majestically through space, trailing luxurious gowns of glimmering light across the night sky. With a crown of radiant light, this Goddess figure is regal and royal, exuding the timeless aura of ancient Egypt. She seems to command the universe as well as fuse with it—a figure in complete harmony with existence.

In *Friendly Aliens* (1990) the same technique of visual reflection and discovery yielded a different emotional tenor. Emerging patterns reminded Kleefeld of tendrils and branches. As she developed those forms, they became whimsical tree-people. Kleefeld emphasizes the branch-like forms that stretch out into surrounding space. Resembling tree limbs, this complex network also alludes to the circulatory system of a higher organism. Carrying allusions to both blood and nerves, they represent life and feeling as general, abstract principles.

Whether figurative or abstract, Kleefeld's *Cosmic Abstractions* are filled with swirling and expansive pictorial energies. They pulse with the rhythm of life. Henry Miller, in discussing the daily journals of Anaïs Nin, astutely chose to emphasize the quality of living energy found in all true works of art:

> A book is a part of life, a manifestation of life, just a much as a tree or a horse or a star. It obeys its own rhythms, its own laws, whether it be a novel, a play, or a diary. The deep, hidden rhythm of life is always there—that of the pulse, the heartbeat. Even in the seemingly stagnant waters of the journal the flux and reflux is evident. It is there in the whole of the work as much as in the fragment. Looked at in its entirety, especially for example in such work as that of Anaïs Nin's, this cosmic pulsation corresponds to the death and rebirth of the individual. Life assumes the aspect of a labyrinth into which the speaker is plunged.[7]

Kleefeld painted the *Cosmic Abstractions* by physically and mentally entering into the canvas and into the full experience of the process. What appeared on the painting was a labyrinth from which both the artist and viewer emerged transformed.

Voodoo Mountain Storm
1990
Acrylic, ink and gouache on canvas
48 x 72 inches

Atoms Mirror Atoms
1990
Acrylic on canvas
48 x 60 inches

1 Gerardus van der Leeuw, *Sacred and Profane Beauty: The Holy in Art* (New York: Abingdon Press, 1963), 11–32.

2 Theodor Schwenk, *Sensitive Chaos: The Creation of Flowing Forms in Water and Air* (London: Rudolf Steiner Press, 1971).

3 Donald Kuspit, "Cosmic Transcendentalism: Surface-Light in John Torreano, Rodney Ripps, and Lynda Benglis," in *The Critic Is Artist: The Intentionality of Art* (Ann Arbor: UMI Research Press, 1984), 217-19.

4 Mircea Eliade, *The Forge and the Crucible: The Origins and Structures of Alchemy* (New York: Harper & Row, 1971).

5 Kleefeld, *Alchemy of Possibility*, 256.

6 William Blake, "Auguries of Innocence" in David V. Erdman, ed., *The Complete Poetry and Prose of William Blake* (New York: Anchor Books, 1988), 490.

7 Henry Miller, "Un Etre Etoilique," in Lawrence Durrell, ed., *The Henry Miller Reader* (New York: New Directions, 1959), 291.

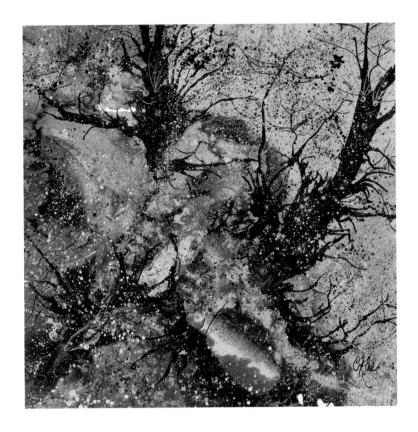

Friendly Aliens
1990
Mixed media on canvas
40 x 40 inches

The Egyptian Space Goddess
1990
Mixed media on canvas
40 x 40 inches

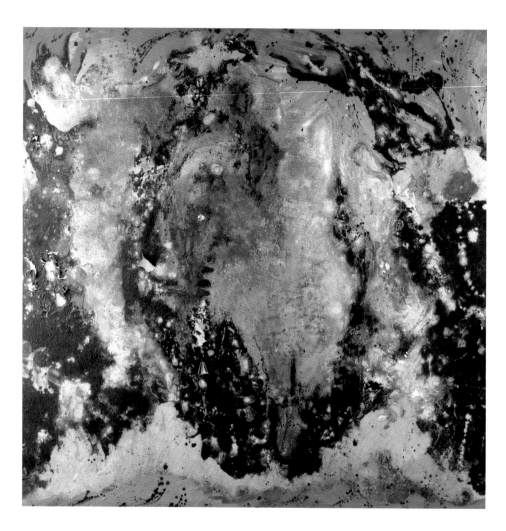

Mountain Impromptu
2006
Mixed media on canvas
30 x 30 inches

Landscape Abstractions

The *Cosmic Abstractions* are essentially landscapes of the universe. Kleefeld also developed a fascinating body of terrestrial landscapes, works in which she interprets the earth around her. But as with all of her art, she does not copy physical reality. Rather she uses the concept of landscape as a starting off point for greater aesthetic and poetic meditations. As seen in *Celestial Mountain* (2006), her landscapes are dynamic images that use paint to conjure the essence or spirit of a locale. In her hands, landscape becomes a vehicle of journey and dream, a way to cross vast spaces and arrive at a fantastic realm that is enriching and emotionally rewarding.

Celestial Mountain is abstract but alludes to a multiplicity of landscape forms. Against a vivid red sky, majestic shapes rise from blue waters. These masses have the presence of great mountains, but unlike static rocks, they twist and flow with seething animal vitality. Peaks rise as powerful pinnacles only to drop dramatically to the depths below. Through these circular movements, the whole painting pulses with rhythmic life. In fact the entire composition is governed by a ceaseless, churning energy, as if Creation were unfolding before our very eyes.

In works such as these, Kleefeld rethinks the very origin of landscape painting. The genre originally served as a way for artists to reflect on the mysteries of the natural world. It should be remembered that the modern conception of landscape—as a faithful copy of a particular place—has been around for only a century and a half. It was not until the advent of Realism and Naturalism in the middle of the 19th century that people came to expect landscape to be a truthful picture of some place specific and real. Before that, landscapes were largely symbolic. From ancient times, well into the Renaissance and Baroque eras, landscape served to capture a general and highly poetic attitude about nature. As exemplified in the fanciful, romantic background of Leonardo da Vinci's *Mona Lisa*, landscape for the vast majority of human history was fictional and imaginary.

Kleefeld also conjures fictitious landscapes. As seen in *Mountain Impromptu* (2006) and *Landscape Transformed* (1990), she looks upon nature more as a force than as a form. Rather than show external appearance, she prefers to delve deep into the inner core to reveal how things live and function. In a way, her conception comes close to the original meaning of the word "nature." Our term derives from the Latin "natura" which originally referred to "the course of things" or "essential character." Kleefeld creates her landscapes by using her materials in an honest way that mirrors the integrity of nature. Pigment stands for earth, medium functions as water, the artist's gesture in space becomes air and energy. Through her frank and spontaneous handling of materials, she acknowledges the continued relevance of the ancient world's four essential elements—earth, water, air and fire.

Celestial Mountain is a towering image that speaks of both heaven and earth. Kleefeld used a great precipice to hint at this fundamental connection between two spheres. Many cultures believe in a "World Mountain," a particular spot that functions as a link to the sacred. It is natural to identify this site with a mound that reaches to the sky, for tall peaks function as ready symbols of spiritual transcendence. Vertical movement captures the

Celestial Mountain
2006
Mixed media on canvas
36 x 36 inches

soul's aspiration for the noble and the exalted. It is not surprising that Kleefeld paints landscapes with great vertical movements. Big Sur is surrounded by mountains. It sits within the Santa Lucia Mountains, a dramatic range in central California that runs along the coast from Monterey to San Luis Obispo. Not far from her home, one can look up to see the inspiring sight of Junipero Serra Peak, the tallest point in the region, which stretches to almost six thousand feet.

While paintings such as *Celestial Mountain* and *Mountain Impromptu* were inspired by dreams of verticality, in other paintings she explored the romance of the horizontal. Most landscapes adhere to this orientation for they often depict an expanse across space. This concept of lateral distance immediately conjures romantic thoughts of journeys and travels. Kleefeld explored these themes in a series of works such as *Dream of Ithaca, Shores of Poseidon,* and *Orphic Mountain Concerto*. These powerfully horizontal paintings bear titles that allude to the Mediterranean world and conjure ideas of voyages to distance lands.

In these paintings Kleefeld returns to an original meaning of the word landscape, which comes from the Dutch and includes a suffix corresponding to the English word "ship." The very term implies a trip across seas and oceans. *Dream of Ithaca* (2005) is long, horizontal, and embodies the notion of travel in its essential structure. It is epic in conception and scope, containing a veritable world within the confines of the rectilinear frame. From a field of glowing blue, gleaming white mountains ascend upwards. They resemble the sea foam from which they emerge, alluding to myths of deities being born from the ocean. Circular, spiraling rhythms capture the feel of a boat rocking upon powerful waves.

Kleefeld has always felt a strong affinity for the land and culture of the Mediterranean. Greece is one of her favorite places on earth. She was drawn to this part of the world not only for its sheer visual beauty but for its lyrical origins. The Greeks have always depended upon the sea. Because the land tends to be dry and rocky, the people have been forced to earn their living from the waters around them. Due to a combination of factors, they tended to live simple, austere lives, focused on meeting their immediate needs through honest work. They learned to respect nature and live in harmony with its eternal rhythms.

Kleefeld has traveled widely throughout her life. She now takes cerebral voyages, aided by her rich store of visual memories and by travel reports of her favorite writers. She especially admires those left by Nikos Kazantzakis. This novelist and man of letters originally turned to travel writing to help earn a living. But he excelled at the art form and is now regarded as a master in the field. Kazantzakis approached travel like a humble pilgrim. Instead of seeking distractions and entertainments, the goals of most tourists, he entered a new region willing to suspend his own worldview. He wanted to learn to see the land through the eyes of a native. In so doing, he gained true insight into the actual spirit of a place. Kleefeld also admired the travel writing of D.H. Lawrence, especially his account of a visit to Italy to visit the Etruscan tombs. His observation that "the true Etruscan quality" involved "ease, naturalness, and an abundance of life, no need to force the mind or the soul in any direction" struck her as a wondrous ideal that captured her own approach to artistic living.[1]

The peoples of the Mediterranean not only lived unaffected lives but also had a true sense for art. Kleefeld celebrates their love for poetry and legend in *Orphic Mountain Concerto* (2007). Orpheus was a figure from Greek mythology regarded as a great singer, poet, and musician. To the ancients, poetry and music were not separate disciplines. Poets sang and often danced their verse in exuberant displays of inspired creativity. The ancient world prized the contributions of their poets, regarding them as cornerstones of their society. Orpheus was so much revered as a pioneer of the civilizing arts that he has also been credited with teaching humanity the art of writing, and even medicine.

Kleefeld's *Orphic Mountain Concerto* (2007) presents a noble and joyous ode to nature. She does not depict Orpheus himself but rather shows mountains moving with a lyrical rhythm. This painting is an

Arcadian idyll and can be seen either as nature inspiring the poet-singer or as Orpheus's song spreading across the hillsides. Either way, there is a unity of landscape and rhythmic vision. Kleefeld rendered this image with a sumptuous array of greens, reds, pinks, and purples, suggesting the richness of rubies and emeralds. Applying paint in small adjacent touches, she created a softer, poetic effect of gently modulated color. The energetic movement of cursive, flowing line and jewel-like color reflects the artist's understanding of the synergistic connection between sight and sound, art and nature. She often paints while listening to music.

Shores of Poseidon (2006) honors another mythic figure, the ancient god of the seas. The structure of this image, with layered bands of color, resembles a Colorfield painting. This movement was pioneered in the 1960s by artists such as Morris Louis, Kenneth Noland, and Helen Frankenthaler. They found a new use for Pollock's method of pouring paint by adopting it to produce large fields of pure, flat color. Classic Colorfield painting is reductive and reticent, offering a beautiful image that is visually appealing but is undemonstrative and emotionally restrained.

Kleefeld unknowingly adopted the look of Colorfield painting but added her own brand of emotion and passion. The alternating bands of color in *Shores of Poseidon* (2006) are anything but neutral and reductive. They pulse and pound with the force of crashing waves. While the blues and greens refer to cool ocean waters and verdant hills, the surprising appearance of blood red serves to underscore the awesome power of the subject. As god of the oceans, Poseidon ruled over a realm that is frightening in its sheer force and unpredictability. Living in Big Sur, Kleefeld is ever aware that calm seas can quickly turn violent. Almost without warning, serene waters can erupt into crushing waves with devastating energy, as if commanded by a bitter and angry god.

In many ways, Big Sur resembles Greece. Both regions consist of rocky, mountainous land surrounded by water. They also share a similar climate. Perhaps because of their closeness to the sea, both places invite a spontaneous and reflective lifestyle. Kleefeld celebrates the similarities between the two regions in *The Pagan Mountains That I Live On* (1989). She sees paganism as a celebration of the single, ever-present spirit that rests behind every religion and every conception of God. She feels this universal spirit as most fully present in the natural world. This painting is rich and replete, bursting with matter and life. It captures the feeling of lightheartedness and weightiness that D.H. Lawrence perceived in the pagan paintings in the ancient Etruscan tombs. He praised the art of the tombs by noting that it is "as natural as life, and yet it has a heavy archaic fullness of meaning."[2] Kleefeld depicts the mountains around Big Sur as infused with the same vital spirit that is solemn and joyous at the same time.

Although the whole of Big Sur often feels like a sacred place, there are times when the soul wishes to retreat into a secret and private realm. She depicts spiritual retreats in *Soul Grotto* (2002) and *Heart Grotto* (2006). A grotto is a natural or artificial cave that has been appropriated by people, often for a special purpose. Because they provide hidden enclosures, grottoes are often associated with romantic or mysterious functions. Over the centuries they have served as homes for mythological beings, as hideaways for smugglers, and as clandestine retreats for lovers. They even have served as chapels, providing a refuge for the faithful.

In Kleefeld's *Heart Grotto* (2006), she depicts a row of stalactites descending from the cave's ceiling. A gap between top and bottom of the grotto is filled with stars. We are within the cave and are looking out into a night sky. But the grotto interior is not simply blank and dark. It is infused with color and light, and glows with an inner radiance. For Kleefeld, the bowels of the earth are as miraculous as the jewel-like stars of the night sky. Representing the internal and the external, as well as the High and the Low, these two realms reveal the extraordinary range and power of the cosmos.

Dream of Ithaca
2005
Ink and acrylic on canvas
36 x 60 inches

Orphic Mountain Concerto
2007
Oil on canvas
36 x 60 inches

In Kleefeld's *Abstract Landscapes* she honors the inner spirit of creation. Her perspective actually has a long lineage in American history. Henry David Thoreau, author of *Walden Pond* and a pioneering naturalist, wrote,

> It is vain to dream of wildness distant from ourselves. There is none such. It is the bog in our brains and bowels, the primitive vigor of Nature in us, that inspires that dream. I shall never find in the wilds of Labrador any greater wildness than in some recess of Concord, i.e. than I import into it.[3]

Henry David Thoreau realized that nature is not a place but a concept. It is an energy and a force, a feeling of naturalness, that exists inside us. Kleefeld follows Thoreau in many ways. Her cliff top home functions as her Concord and her Walden Pond. It is a microcosm that allows her to see and appreciate the grand macrocosm that is the cosmos. As Thoreau realized, the act of seeing nature entails greater involvement on our part than most people realize or admit. It is our active participation that gives nature its true grandeur and epic quality.

---

1   D. H. Lawrence, "Etruscan Places" in *D.H. Lawrence and Italy,* (New York: Penguin Books, 1972), 12.

2   Lawrence, "Etruscan Places," 36.

3   Henry David Thoreau, Journal, August 30, 1856, quoted in Simon Schama, *Landscape and Memory* (New York: Vintage Books, 1996), frontispiece.

Soul Grotto
2002
Oil on canvas
36 x 36 inches

Shores of Poseidon
2006
Oil on canvas
48 x 60 inches

Heart Grotto
2006
Oil on canvas
48 x 60 inches
Artist's Dedication: "In beloved
memory of Dorris Halsey"

The Pagan Mountains that I Live On
1989
Mixed media on board
32 x 40 inches

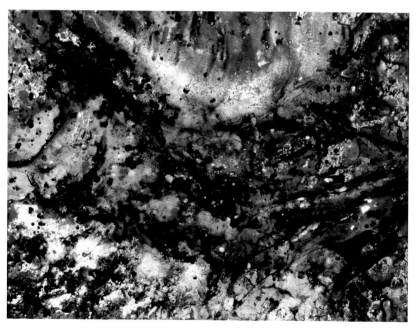

Landscape Transformed
1990
Mixed media on board
31 x 40.5 inches

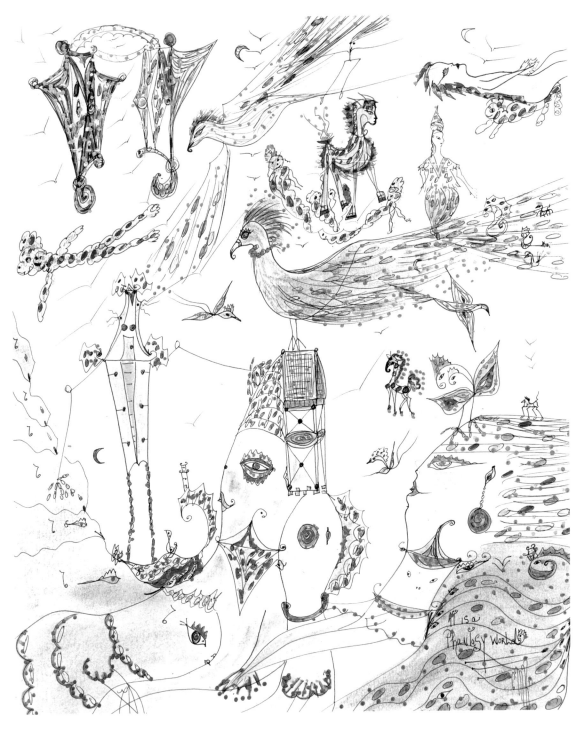

It is a Phantasy World
1992
Pastel and colored pen on paper
17 x 14 inches

Linear Fantasies

In the early 1990s, Kleefeld embarked on a new direction in her art. She began to explore line. Line is one of the most curious and paradoxical elements in art. It is a fundamental part of visual images but rests on a grand illusion. As they say in art schools, "there are no lines in nature." Real objects have only edges and boundaries; nothing exists with an outline around it. Lines are invented to describe forms and ideas. They are fictional constructs that allow artists to create a pictorial world that parallels our own.

This is exactly how Kleefeld embarked on her new *Linear Fantasies*. She used line to create an alternate universe. These images are grand in scope, encompassing entire realms. As seen in *Living Space* (1993) and *Reflections Are More Interesting* . . . (1993), the subject is a fully functional world. While earlier paintings were largely flat, there is a new sense of implied depth. People and things relate to each other within shallow, stage-like spaces. As on a stage, what unfolds is a human drama, as funny and as moving as life itself.

To create this new body of work, Kleefeld abandoned the scale of her large *Cosmic Abstractions* and began to work small. The physical demands of painting while bending and stooping placed a strain on her back. She returned to making art while sitting down. Rather than actively dripping paint, she also employed new tools—pastel and pen. Pastel is a dry medium. It is manufactured in sticks of compressed dry pigment and is designed to produce a powdery swath of color. Every stroke leaves a rich deposit of intense and saturated color. It is like drawing with pure pigment.

But Kleefeld did not use pastel in the usual manner. Always eager to test the limits and capacity of her media, she experimented with rubbing pigment into the surface of the paper. In this manner, pigment and paper became one. The surface exudes a pale, colored light. The visual effect is not unlike the late watercolors of the English landscape painter J.M.W. Turner where thin washes of color capture the soft glow of early morning radiance.

Upon this field of gently luminous color, Kleefeld rendered her image with pen and ink. Using a sharply pointed instrument, she created a filigree of thin black lines that move with an emphatic grace. They flow, twist, and turn in gorgeous arabesques. In fact, her marks are best described as a form of pictorial calligraphy—a fitting mode for a poet-artist. One is reminded of Paul Klee's famous description of a line as a thought taking a walk. Kleefeld's line moves with the same lyric and fluid energy. The incisive quality of her lines rivets our attention, coaxing the eye to follow wherever they lead. Line wanders and meanders gracefully as it generates a host of simple, primal symbols that we interpret as a person or an animal or a house. As in her youthful *Nanose*, these invented people and things are beguiling in their child-like simplicity.

The analogy to the work of the Bauhaus artist Paul Klee is particularly fitting. Kleefeld felt a keen affinity with this modern master and for a period of time signed her name with the shortened form: "Carolyn Klee." Both Kleefeld and Klee see the world as a place of magic and whimsy. Paul Klee created images that pass for the workings of a vast cosmic machine. Kleefeld also sees the world as a wondrously fantastic place, like a grand stage set or a fabulous timepiece run by a cosmic clockmaker.

Going to See Pops
1993
Pastel and colored pen on paper
17 x 14 inches

Kleefeld not only altered her media but also changed her subject matter. Her early works from the 1980s were about symbol and process. The *Linear Fantasies* address a new theme—narrative. Each one tells a story. Narrative has had an enduring role in art because it is so engaging. Narrative art places an individual within a flow of events. It is the one art form that captures the dynamic flow of real time. Action becomes real and tangible.

There was one key episode that inspired this series—the aging and death of her father, Mark Taper. A strong and powerful man throughout his life, Taper began to grow frail in the late 1980s. As one who always focused on his businesses, he never quite understood Carolyn's interest in art and poetry, activities that had little material gain. As a result of their differing points of view, they had grown apart as adults and for years were not particularly close. But as his health deteriorated, she began to actively care for him. A new bond developed between father and daughter.

She remembers that as his failing memory became worse, he lost the iron-clad will that drove him to the top of the business world. He became softer, gentler, and more accepting. Carolyn was able to see her father as someone other than the commanding and controlling titan of industry. He became a loved and loving human being, a newly born, gentle soul. As one might presume, this period was one of great emotional upheaval for her. But these works show little hint of sadness or loss. She painted them as an expression of the healing and union between her father and herself.

Going to See Pops (1993) represents one of the many trips she made from Big Sur to visit her father in Beverly Hills. The artist depicts herself as a horse, her favorite alter-ego, and a memory of her childhood pet, Mabel. She is shown with a drawing on her lap. In fact, many of these ink and pastel drawings were executed riding in a car while making these journeys. She is surrounded by a host of whimsical creatures—fantastic birds, playful cloud-lambs—that guide her on her path.

Kleefeld celebrates the transformative nature of color in *The Blue Haired Guardians* (1992). She sees blue as a symbol of innocence and beauty. It stands for devotion and gentleness, qualities she was experiencing in a relationship at the time. This image was also influenced by Marc Chagall who used blue as a color of poetic transcendence.

At the time, Kleefeld wrestled with philosophical questions such as: What constitutes reality? Every moment we are presented with a wealth of sensory data. How do we know what is real? When two people experience the same event and draw two different conclusions, whose reality is more correct? She addressed these themes in *Exterior Appearance* (1993) and *It is a Phantasy World* (1992). These works reflect her understanding of the provisional character of the real. To her, reality is always based on personal perspective and is only a subjective appearance.

One way to gain deeper understanding of the world we live in is by sharing experiences. We all mirror and reflect one another. This is the theme of *Reflections Are More Interesting...* (1993) and *We Are Reflections of Each Other* (1993). The latter was owned by Dr. Timothy Leary, a friend of the artist. Kleefeld feels that we were all put on this earth to help one another however we can. The scenes she depicts all occur in places of social interaction. Although no specific locations are described, we have the sense of city streets or domestic interiors. Intimate spaces such as living rooms, bedrooms, parlors, even streets, are places defined by the human relations that occur there. It is the animating energy of the figures that gives these spaces life and resonance. As Gaston Bachelard wrote, "our house is our corner of our world. As has often been said, it is our first universe, a real cosmos in every sense of the word."[1]

These ink and pastel drawings are also enlivened by a whimsical use of patterning. The surface of the paper is covered with various types of ornament. The decorative shapes—curlicues, glyphs, dots and dashes—were all

The Blue Haired Guardians
1992
Pastel and colored pens on paper
14 x 17 inches

Exterior Appearance
1993
Pastel and colored pen on paper
14 x 17 inches

rendered spontaneously by the artist's quickly roaming pen. These inventive symbols are written as much as drawn and form a highly personal, graphic language. This delight in elaborate, all-over decoration is known by the Latin term, *horror vacui*, or fear of emptiness. Her obsessive desire to fill her paper with a vast array of marks and patterns reflects her deep love for the fascinating complexity of the world and its expanding infinity. It also reflects a sense of care and dedication—an extension of the attention she was showing to her ailing father at the time.

While most of the *Linear Fantasies* were executed small-scale on paper, Kleefeld did adopt this imagery to create a few large-scale canvases such as *Spying Through Time* (1992) and *Cosmic Cartoon* (1993). *Spying Through Time* is a fantastic composition of fanciful and whimsical creatures. The central figure, a strange, jolly cloud-man, is surrounded by various invented beasts. Familiar yet strange, these animals seem like fish, birds, and mammals all at once. The range of species knows no limits in this free-wheeling mélange of joyous vitality. The large central figure is smiling. In ancient, pre-classical art, this type of expression was known as the "Archaic smile." Although the exact meaning is unknown, it is generally believed that this smile was used to create a sense of health and well-being. This emphatic smile radiates joy and signals that all is well with the world.

Another large *Linear Fantasy* is *Cosmic Cartoon*. The mention of a cartoon refers to both high and low art. In art history, a cartoon is a preliminary study. A key part of artistic practice during the Renaissance, cartoons were full-scale drawings created by an artist to resolve pictorial problems before commencing the final work. In popular culture, a cartoon refers to a form of humorous entertainment, either a comic strip or animated film, designed to amuse and delight. Kleefeld's painting functions as a traditional cartoon in that it offers a study or sketch for life. It is also funny, reflecting her observation that the wonders of the everyday world are too ironic to be taken too seriously. Her *Linear Fantasies* follow the tradition of our great humorist authors, such as Jonathan Swift, Lewis Carroll, and Edward Lear, who fabricated whole worlds based on cosmic irony. The power of their humor derived from their ability to invent entire imaginary worlds and make them seem plausible, if not real.

Despite the prevailing light-hearted mood of the *Linear Fantasies*, it must be remembered that Kleefeld fabricated these works while coping with her father's final illness. When Mark Taper died at his home on Thursday, December 15, 1994, at the age of 91, Kleefeld lost a father and the world lost a great businessman, philanthropist, and humanitarian. The experience of caring for him in his last years moved her to tell stories once again. John Dunne, a Catholic theologian, wrote a perceptive book entitled *Time and Myth: A Meditation on Storytelling as an Exploration of Life and Death*.[2] He argued that life and death are not absolute states but points on a grand voyage. This trip occurs through time and space, involving a sequence of unfolding events. The wonders of this journey and the resulting story give depth and meaning to life.

---

1   Gaston Bachelard, *The Poetics of Space* (New York: The Orion Press, 1964), 4.
2   John S. Dunne, *Time and Myth: A Meditation on Storytelling as an Exploration of Life and Death* (Notre Dame, IN: University of Notre Dame Press, 1975).

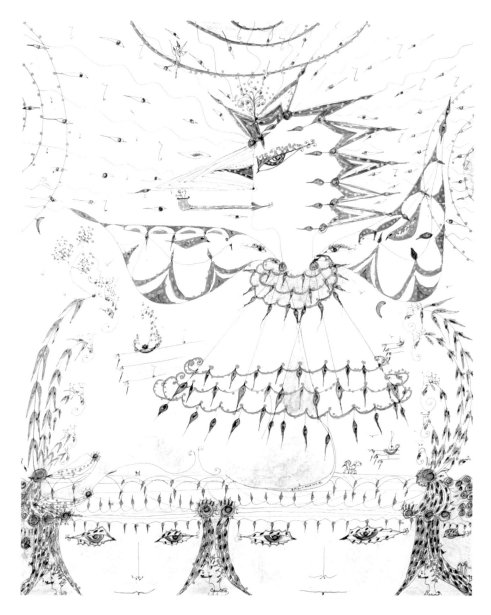

Ambivalence
1993
Pastel and colored pen on paper
17 x 14 inches

Living Space
1993
Pastel and colored ink on paper
17 x 14 inches

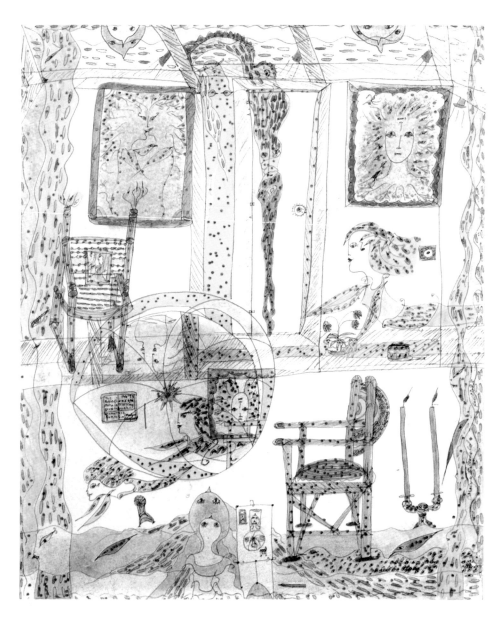

Reflections Are More Interesting . . .
1993
Pastel and colored ink on paper
17 x 14 inches

We Are Reflections of Each Other
1993
Pastel and colored ink on paper
14 x 17 inches

Spying Through Time
1992
Acrylic and ink on canvas
48 x 48 inches

Cosmic Cartoon
1993
Mixed media on canvas
48 x 48 inches

Lovers in Metamorphosis
1999
Oil on canvas
30 x 24 inches

Lovers

Art is love in creation and love is an art created.

May we create relationships as we would create art, continually reinventing ourselves in the process, using our imagination rather than society's stereotypes to express our ideals.
—Carolyn Mary Kleefeld[1]

Kleefeld is fascinated by that curious emotion called "love," and she has addressed the theme in whole collections of paintings and poems. Love is, naturally, an everlasting theme that has preoccupied human beings since time immemorial. In the 1960s it became a cultural issue. The newly emerging youth movement rallied around love as the standard of anti-materialist and anti-establishment values. The great gathering of young people in San Francisco in 1967 to promote a new, spiritual outlook was called the Summer of Love.[2] In the 1970s this interest in personal love became mainstream and manifested itself in an ethos of sexual liberation. At the same time psychologists explored the depths of interpersonal relationships. Erich Fromm, a social psychologist and humanistic philosopher, wrote the popular book *The Art of Loving* in 1956. In 1972 Leo Buscaglia published a book with the simple title *Love*. This instant bestseller was promoted as "a warm and wonderful book about the largest experience in life."[3]

In her *Lovers* series, begun in the late 1990s, Kleefeld explored the vast power of love to alter perceptions, transform lives, and open new worlds. *Butterfly Lovers* (1998) typifies the magical element that runs through these works. In a dream-like landscape, two fairy-like figures cavort in an open meadow. Miraculously, their arms have transformed into wings. The standing male figure has blue skin and wears a crown, a sign of royalty. The female figure is pink and reclines with glorious ease. Vertical and horizontal, they symbolize opposing yet symbiotic masculine and feminine energies. Balancing polarities is an essential theme for Kleefeld, and she has stated that "Opposites are dynamic interplayers essential to evolution."[4] Kleefeld shows these lovers participating in a dignified and timeless rite, one with a lineage that stretches back for millennia and will continue as long as humans inhabit this planet. They are visited by a joyous bird that indicates this scene is elemental and rooted in primal nature.

Instead of fusing into a single entity, these figures maintain their physical separateness, barely touching at their lower legs. This symbolizes an essential factor of mature love—independence. Immature love is often marked by a neediness where one person depends too much and develops too strong an attachment for the other. A healthy, mature relationship ackknowledges, respects, and celebrates the uniqueness of each person. Adult love aspires to self-actualization.

Kleefeld's lovers dwell in a space that resembles a garden. As Simon Schama perceptively noted, "Eden was a garden, not a forest."[5] The difference is vital. Forests may be towering, impenetrable, and tend to intimidate with their size and antiquity, making humans feel small and insignificant. Gardens are accessible, welcoming, and inviting. They are created by people for people. By placing the lovers in a garden-like setting, Kleefeld

Butterfly Lovers
1998
Oil on canvas
30 x 36 inches

makes an important point that love is something we must cultivate. Love requires care and nurturing in order to survive and thrive. As Erich Fromm observed, "To love means to commit oneself without guarantee . . . . Love is an act of faith."[6]

Lovers in Metamorphosis (1999) offers a more fantastic image, a veritable symphony for the senses. As the title indicates, love is a transforming experience, one with the power to magically change people. Everything is unstable, in a state of flux or transformation. Against a deep red sky, two lovers float and touch at the cheek. Their multi-colored wings resemble clouds as well as the butterflies that hover around them. Other symbols of cultural refinement—architecture and a musical instrument—hint that the lofty experience of love is natural but also an art, one that takes skilled and sensitive practitioners. The lovers experience a profound metamorphosis from chrysalis to butterfly—among Kleefeld's favorite metaphors. In *The Cloud Dreamers* (2000), the figures also have been transported to the ethereal realm of the sky. Kleefeld sees her paintings as "daydreams from the wilderness of the unconscious."

In the ancient world, love was often symbolized by cupids. Whether depicted as pudgy babies or young boys, they are always youthful and immature. Kleefeld's figures are clearly adult. They also tend to assume elongated, lozenge forms. These shapes, organic but sharply tapering, end in an emphatic point. The sharp pointed arrows of Cupid have been transformed into the figures themselves. Mature lovers do not require sharp jabs to be awakened to love; rather, feelings emerge from the core of their being.

The English word "love" is inadequate to capture the limitless range of powerful and nuanced emotions humans experience in love. The ancient Greeks differentiated no less than five distinct meanings of love. "Agape" refers to a noble, ideal type of love and has been translated as "love of the soul." "Eros" is passionate love, filled with desire and longing. To refer to a lofty, virtuous love, the Greeks used the term "phila," which encompasses love for friends and community. "Storge" conveys the idea of a natural affection, such as that of family members for each other. "Xenia" implies the sense of hospitality that occurs between total strangers.

Kleefeld's *Lovers* series captures the full range of these experiences, running the gamut from platonic caring to passionate attraction. Soon after Kleefeld published her first collection of poems, *Climates of the Mind*, in 1980, she received a letter from a reader conveying his admiration for that book. Eventually she invited that fan, David Wayne Dunn, to become a poet in residence in Big Sur. When Dunn arrived, the two realized it had been seventeen years to the day since he had written his first letter. Subsequently, a special romance developed between the two, and in 2003 they published their poems in *Kissing Darkness*, a collection capturing their complex and mutually inspiring relationship, which Kleefeld sees as "catalytically creative."

Circus Lovers (2000) offers a meditation on two distinct types of love—romantic and artistic. This painting is an homage to Mark Chagall, the School of Paris painter who created entire fantasy worlds based on his own life. Kleefeld greatly values artists with the vision and courage to break free from conventions and conceive new realities, and thus she has special admiration for Chagall's originality, spirituality and idealism.

The universal power of love is beyond doubt. But what is its relation to art? History tells us that love is the source of art. The ancient Greeks attributed the origins of painting to a young woman of Rhodes. When her lover prepared to leave on a long voyage, she took a piece of charcoal from the hearth and while he lay asleep drew the outline of his shadow on the wall. She had produced an image of her love that would endure his absence. In the process, she created art. This notion of a close link between art and love persists today. When Henry Miller wrote an essay on his own painting it bore the title: "To Paint Is to Love Again."[7] Kleefeld also experiences painting itself as a great love affair—a passionate involvement with the fullness of life.

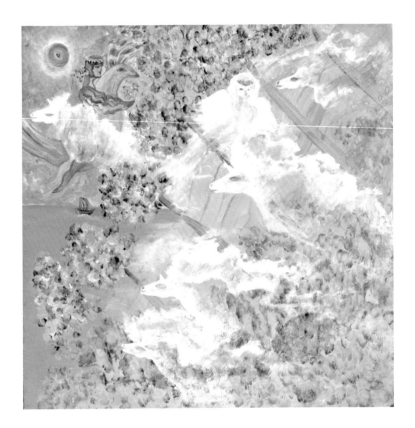

The Cloud Dreamers
2000
Oil on canvas
20 x 20 inches

1   Carolyn Mary Kleefeld, *Soul Seeds* (Merrick, NY: Cross-Cultural Communications, 2008), 48, 51.

2   Christoph Grunenberg, ed., *Summer of Love: Art of the Psychedelic Era* (London: Tate Publishing, 2005).

3   Leo Buscaglia, *Love* (New York: Fawcett Crest, 1982).

4   Kleefeld, *Alchemy of Possibility*, 111.

5   Simon Schama, *Landscape and Memory* (New York: Vintage Books, 1995), 226.

6   Erich Fromm, *The Art of Loving* (London: Unwin Paperback, 1979), 105.

7   Henry Miller, *To Paint is to Love Again* (Alhambra, CA: Cambria Books, 1960).

Circus Lovers
2000
Oil on canvas
24 x 18 inches

Moon Angels
1999
Oil on canvas
36 x 30 inches

The Moon Bathers
1999
Oil on canvas
36 x 30 inches

Goddess Wearing the Mountain
1999
Oil on canvas
24 x 18 inches

The Goddess and the Paradise Garden

Many visitors to Big Sur stop at Julia Pfeiffer Burns State Park. Covering almost 2,000 acres, this park encompasses an astonishing variety of terrain, ranging from coast to canyons. The scenery, which includes pristine beaches as well as palm trees and groves of majestic redwoods, is breathtaking at every turn. McWay Falls features a waterfall that drops eighty feet directly into the ocean below and is regarded as among the most picturesque sights in the nation.

Kleefeld was inspired by this place to create a group of intimate paintings devoted to the theme of idyllic nature. In *Haven at Julia's* (1996), a very small work, Kleefeld conjures an entire world. The artist depicts herself as a red-headed woman sitting at a seaside cove. She has always felt the rocky terrain of Big Sur to be reminiscent of the lyrical beauty of Greece. In this work, a sentinel bird watches as she launches a boat, a symbol of life's voyage. Above them, a tree bursts into a riot of mandala-shaped leaves. On the distant mountains stands an exotic, pagoda-like building. The scene is one of lyric communing with nature where flora and fauna, nature and culture, all exist in a peaceful, symbiotic relationship.

This series depicts what may be called a paradise garden. The phrase derives from the ancient Persian and originally referred to a special, walled-in enclave. These luxurious gardens were renowned throughout the ancient world as offering abundance and exquisite beauty. Containing a pool or fountain, surrounded by wondrous and exotic plants, such a self-enclosed and self-sustaining realm provides a perfect retreat from the ills and trials of reality beyond the walls. For Kleefeld, Big Sur best approximates this idyllic, magical place, and she addressed the theme in other works such as *Red Bird Seeds* (2000).

Spirit Bird Tower of Julia Pfeiffer Burns (1996) and *Spirit Pavilion of Julia Pfeiffer Burns* (1996) convey the idea of the house as a spiritual retreat. These fanciful structures resemble towers of contemplation and celebrate the healing, transformative energy dwelling in the home. Bearing candle-like flames that radiate light and power, these structures can be thought of as celestial temples. In his book, *The Poetics of Space*, Gaston Bachelard maintained that the house is a special place that invites the soul to turn inward.[1] These intimate domestic spaces offer a quiet refuge from the noise and chaos of the external world.

Kleefeld investigates the idea of her home as a spiritual retreat in *Soul Haven* (1999) and *Cosmic Temple* (2005). Although it is consecrated by no formal religious authority, her home is a powerfully spiritual place for Kleefeld. Its connection to the sacred emerges from its sense of rootedness, a deep emotion captured in *Casa de la Duende* (1999). In South American folklore, the word "duende" refers to a fairy-like creature. The Spanish poet Federico García Lorca introduced the literary and artistic use of the word in an address in 1930. He defined the term as referring to a powerful but ineffable quality, a special feeling of profundity or soulfulness. Kleefeld has always valued this artistic ideal.

A complex and complicated emotion, duende combines two opposites—an exuberant celebration of life combined with an acknowledgement of the presence of death. Duende is happy and sad, joyous and melancholy, a recognition of both our infinite spirit and our finite, mortal body. In *Casa de la Duende* Kleefeld

Haven at Julia's
1996
Oil on canvas
12 x 9 inches

Red Bird Seeds
2000
Oil on canvas
14 x 11 inches

Gypsy Spirit of the Sea
2002
Oil on canvas
24 x 12 inches

Spirit Bird Tower of Julia Pfeiffer Burns
1996
Oil on canvas
12 x 9 inches

depicts her home as an altar or ziggurat, surmounted by an all-seeing eye, a symbol of the great emotional depths contained within.

The bird that figures prominently in *Haven at Julia's* (1996) and *Spirit Bird Tower of Julia Pfeiffer Burns* (1996) carries special meaning for the artist. Kleefeld maintains an outdoor aviary at her home and feels at one with the birds. They symbolize flight and freedom. She spends times with them and knows their nuanced personality traits and moods and finds that, although they are different from humans on the evolutionary scale, they are just like people, and share our lives in rich, symbiotic relationships. One of her birds sometimes perches on her shoulder while she paints.

In these paintings, Kleefeld depicted herself as a princess or a goddess, as a woman possessing rare and fine inner gifts. Like other works in this series, *Gypsy Spirit of the Sea* (2002) and *Goddess Wearing the Mountain* (1999) are symbolic self-portraits. Certain features—the red hair and tall, lean physique—reflect Kleefeld's own physical appearance. But these figures are shown larger-than-life because the artist sees herself as one and the same with nature.

The Women's Movement of the 1970s revived interest in the goddess figure. The earliest cultures saw a distinction between masculine and feminine powers and honored goddesses to celebrate a female sensibility that is intuitive, nurturing, and creative. Women generate and sustain life from the fiber of their own bodies and function as vital forces of nature.

Goddess Wearing the Mountain shows the artist as a glorious, feminine profile floating above the hills, signaling an essential bond between her and the universe. She is part of nature and transcends it through her own will and spirit. Kleefeld sees her life's work in terms of continuing—and transforming—the matriarchal order of her ancestors. As she explained,

> I also inherited a lineage of oppressed females on my mother's side, some of whom committed suicide. My mother's German mother was not allowed downstairs until her less attractive sisters were married. My mother's feeling of resignation in giving up her art career to have children had a profound effect on my resolve to live differently. I feel my drive for artistic expression is partially propelled by my mother, that I am in a sense liberating my female ancestors today from what they suffered yesterday.[2]

While Amelia Taper chose to suppress her artistic nature, her youngest daughter has allowed it to emerge and sing out in full voice. Through her art, Kleefeld honors her female ancestors and at the same time breaks free from generations of social oppression. Her paintings and writings offer an alternative vision of exuberant creativity and spiritual freedom.

---

1   Gaston Bachelard, *The Poetics of Space* (New York: The Orion Press, 1964).

2   Kleefeld, *Alchemy of Possibility*, 224.

Spirit Pavilion of Julia Pfeiffer Burns
1996
Oil on canvas
9 x 12 inches

Soul Haven
1999
Oil on canvas
11 x 14 inches

Casa de la Duende
1999
Oil on canvas
9 x 12 inches

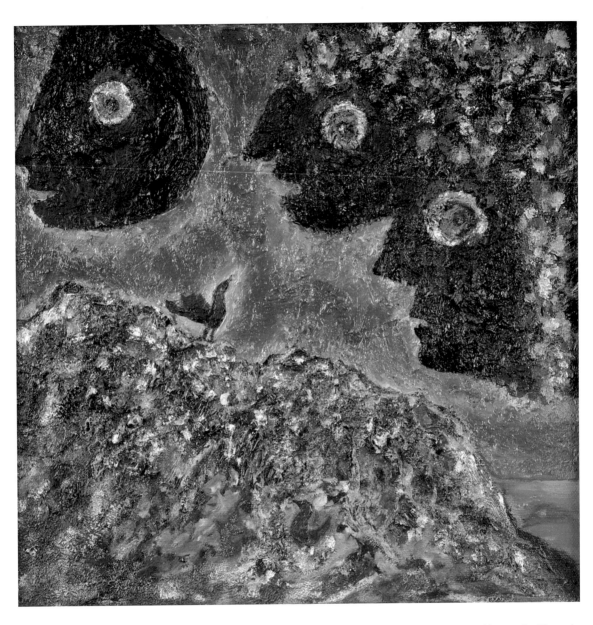

Mountain Alvernia
2003
Oil on canvas
12 x 12 inches

Saint Francis

Carolyn Kleefeld is drawn to art based on instincts fueling powerful passions. In 2003, she created a small series of paintings based on the life of Saint Francis. Although they are of modest dimensions, these images rank among her most striking and thought-provoking in terms of sheer emotional intensity.

The word saint derives from the Latin "sanctus" and refers to the holy. People designated as saints are thought to live especially holy lives and convey in their mortal body the presence of God. In the 20th century, a number of secular intellectuals turned to saints for what they tell us about human nature and the noble search for high ideals. Psychologist Rollo May once wrote about "the poets of the religious sphere we call saints."[1] He saw saints as exemplifying a rare breed of creative beings. Like poets, they are driven by inspiration to defy convention and pursue their own visionary impulses. Aldous Huxley saw saints as individuals caught in an existential crisis of good and evil,

> The saint is one who knows that every moment of our human life is a moment of crisis; for at every moment we are called upon to make an all-important decision—to choose between the way that leads to death and spiritual darkness and the way that leads towards light and life; between interests exclusively temporal and the eternal order; between our personal will, or the will of some projection of our personality, and the will of God.[2]

Another writer who embraced the question of sainthood was Nikos Kazantzakis, the Greek poet, novelist and essayist, and one of Kleefeld's favorite authors. Kazantzakis wrote *Saint Francis* and *The Last Temptation of Christ*, two novels that retell the stories of key figures from Christian history and theology. In *Saint Francis*, he presents the life of the beloved Catholic saint as a creative seeker and spiritual pilgrim. He presents the saint as a profoundly real man who is beset by doubt and uncertainty and who is driven by a restless need for truth and deep meaning.

Kleefeld offers her own interpretation of this spiritual search in *The Crucibles of Saint Francis* (2003). A crucible is a cup or container usually used to melt metals at extremely high temperatures. Crucibles aid in the transformation of materials but remain unchanged. Alchemists used crucibles in their attempts to transform base metals into gold. Kleefeld sees Saint Francis's mortal body and life as a crucible. It is a medium for affecting a more glorious spiritual conversion. In the painting, he appears rising above the mortals who remain earthbound below him.

The painting *San Damiano* (2003) depicts the church near Assisi, Italy, where Francis first saw a vision of Christ. While he was praying within this dilapidated structure, a carved crucifix came to life and ordered him to repair the church. Francis later realized that Christ meant for him to reform and renew the entire Catholic faith. This vision led Francis to create a new order that would be known as the Franciscans. Kleefeld interprets this vision in a powerful and passionate abstract composition.

Mountain Alvernia (2003) shows the place where Francis received the stigmata. Kleefeld represents the scene in an original way, using a bird to symbolize the plight of Francis, who is earthbound but yearns to be

Ascent of Saint Francis
2003
Oil on canvas
14 x 18 inches

The Crucibles of Saint Francis
2003
Oil on canvas
30 x 30 inches

San Damiano
2003
Oil on canvas
12 x 12 inches

unified with the beyond. The three faces hovering in the glowing fire-red sky symbolize the Trinity. Both Kazantzakis and Kleefeld saw Francis's religious dilemmas as struggles not with heaven, but with the polarities in the world. It was by wrestling with the concrete problems of life on earth that Francis truly experienced and reached the divine.

This ultimate goal is shown in *Ascent of Saint Francis* (2003). The saint has wings and begins his upwards flight. Kleefeld identifies closely with birds and sees them as symbols of liberation and freedom. In a fascinating passage, D. H. Lawrence explained the relationship of birds and churches:

> The Holy Spirit is a Dove, or an Eagle. In the Old Testament it was an Eagle; in the New Testament it is a Dove. And there are, standing over the Christian world, the Churches of the Dove and the Churches of the Eagle….the Churches of the Eagle stand high, with their heads to the skies, as if they challenged the world below. They are the Churches of the spirit of David, and their bells ring passionately, imperiously, falling on the subservient world below.[3]

Kleefeld chose to depict Saint Francis as an eagle, as a powerful being who uses inner strength and resolve to rise above the mundane Earth and reach the holy.

In her art she focuses on transforming matter into spirit. Her artistic process uses experiences as mulch for new insights that expand our awareness and open up whole new worlds of creative possibility.

---

1   Rollo May, *The Courage to Create*, (New York: Norton, 1975), 22.

2   Aldous Huxley, *The Perennial Philosophy* (New York: Harper & Brothers, 1945), 43.

3   D. H. Lawrence, "The Spinner and the Monk" in *D.H. Lawrence and Italy*, (New York: Penguin Books, 1972), 19.

Trees of Carolyn and David
1999
Oil on canvas
18 x 24 inches

Trees and Landscapes

I would not get rid of my feelings by copying the tree exactly or by drawing the leaves one by one in the current idiom . . . Only after I have identified myself with it. I have to create an object that resembles the tree. The symbol of the tree.
—Henri Matisse [1]

Over the years Kleefeld has painted many trees, returning often to the subject. Like Matisse, she identifies with them on a personal level and renders their forms as compelling symbols. It is not surprising she would cherish this theme since trees are an important part of her environment and her life. Her home is located at the end of a road winding through a dense grove of sequoias. These ancient redwoods stand as silent sentinels that guard the scene while holding eternal secrets locked within their towering trunks. Out of the thick woods and beyond a clearing, her home is surrounded by smaller trees which function as a modest break against almost ceaseless onshore winds.

Kleefeld communes with these trees daily. They serve as a constant reminder of the power of nature alive. She finds them so fascinating in part because they provide a mirror of ourselves. They stand erect with their heads high in the air. Their roots reach deep into the soil, and one can say they keep their feet on the ground. They possess limbs and appear to have the capacity to touch and embrace. In a curious way, trees resemble people more than most animals.

In 1994, Kleefeld produced a small but striking group of paintings presenting the tree as a symbol of life, death, and cosmic time. Poetic titles capture the rich and resonant aura of these paintings: *Dead Tree at Pankosmion, Gemini Moon, Golden Eye of the Janus Tree,* and *Taurean Moon.*

Dead Tree at Pankosmion depicts a specific tree at Kleefeld's home. As she explained, the word "pankosmion" is "from the Greek, meaning 'place of the whole universe,' the name of my mountaintop home, a Garden of Eden where the chrysalis is ever becoming the butterfly, where the guardians protect the soul's treasures."[2] This small canvas is oval, alluding to the rich, sumptuous decorative art of the 18th-century Rococo. The theme, however, is anything but light-hearted. At the center of the composition stands a gnarled, twisted, and blighted old tree. This venerable and noble creature has died and is rendered with pure black, the color of mourning. Yet it is surrounded by lush plants in the artist's garden that have burst out in flower. This rich array of joyous, riotous colors celebrates the renewal of life.

The theme of time continues in *Gemini Moon* and *Taurean Moon.* They depict trees in Asian settings and make a knowing reference to the forms of traditional Japanese art, with flattened forms in a condensed, two-dimensional space. Bold red borders are filled with abstract symbols that resemble characters from Japanese writing. The titles refer to astrological signs. Astrology is based on the belief that the movements of celestial bodies have an effect on terrestrial affairs. For Kleefeld, this ancient discipline is only part of her conviction that the entire universe is governed by larger and ever-expanding rhythms and patterns. She often cites the alchemical saying, "As above, so below," as a statement of her belief that everything in the cosmos is related to everything else. *Gemini Moon* and *Taurean Moon* offer a romantic meditation on the universal and timeless character of trees, which can persist through different time periods, in different cultures, and in different parts of the world, and still maintain their integrity.

Golden Eye of the Janus Tree pays respect to the enduring wisdom of trees. Trees are older than humans and contain ancient knowledge. Janus was the Roman god of change and transition. Usually depicted with two heads looking in opposing directions, he symbolized endings that are also beginnings. In central California there are ancient giant redwoods that are believed to date back to the time of Christ. Because of their great antiquity, they function as symbols of the timeless. They stood in the distant past and, hopefully, will stand in the future. They look forward and back over the course of human events, exuding an aura of impassive certainty and inherent nobility.

Trees also serve as signs of religious transcendence, as seen in *Trees on the Summit of Sinai* (2003). With roots that reach below the soil and limbs that stretch towards the sky, they serve as apt bridges between heaven and earth. One must remember that the ancient Greeks gathered in groves deemed to be sacred. Celtic and Germanic tribes worshipped in deep, dark forests. Their pagan tree cults honored the annual regeneration of life. The symbolic power of trees was even acknowledged in the Judeo-Christian tradition. At the center of the Garden of Eden stood the Tree of Life. God spoke to Moses through a tree that burned but was not consumed, a momentous event Kleefeld honored in her painting, *Trees on the Summit of Sinai* (2003). In the medieval era Gothic cathedrals were erected with interiors hinting at the ambiance of a sacred forest. All these traditions point to the tree as a symbol of the holy on earth.

The pure romance of trees is captured in *Trees of Carolyn and David* (1999) which is a song of love. The man in the painting is David Wayne Dunn, with whom Carolyn shares a mutually-inspired love of and passion for art, poetry, and music. Kleefeld and Dunn celebrated their life together in their book, *Kissing Darkness: Love Poems and Art*, which consists of poems and art created by each of them during the first years of their relationship.

Edmund's Tree Song (2001) uses trees to honor another important relation in Kleefeld's life— Edmund Kara, a dear friend and neighbor who passed away in that year. She remembers him as an artist and esthete who lived an admirable ascetic life dedicated to simplicity and beauty. Although he had enjoyed a successful career as a fashion designer and interior decorator in Hollywood, he moved to Big Sur in the 1960s to devote his life to his sculpture. He lived in a studio on a precipitous cliff just below Kleefeld's home, and she often made her way down the incline to his modest cabin. She fondly recalls the hours they spent sitting in his austere but exquisite living room, philosophizing about life, as they watched the sunset. He advocated a life of detachment, rejecting possessions as well as society's expectations, in order to live each moment fully and in the present. When she first moved to Big Sur, Kara was an inspiring influence, and over the years he continued to be a guiding spirit, offering a living example of a liberated existence.

Living in Big Sur, Kara focused his attention on making extraordinary wood sculpture. Often, friends noticed fascinating pieces of felled wood on the shore or in forests that they would bring to Kara to serve as raw material. From the natural beauty of the trees around him, he made greater beauty. *Edmund's Tree Song* celebrates a reconnection to primal existence and to the eternal play of life and art, nature and culture, which is a constant source of renewal.

---

1   Henri Matisse, "Letter to Aragon," in Marie-France Boyer, *Matisse at Villa Le Réve* (New York: Thames and Hudson, 2004), 100.

2   Kleefeld, *Alchemy of Possibility*, 257.

Trees on the Summit of Sinai
2003
Oil on canvas
16 x 12 inches

Golden Eye of the Janus Tree
1994
Enamel and metallic gouache on canvas
10 x 8 inches

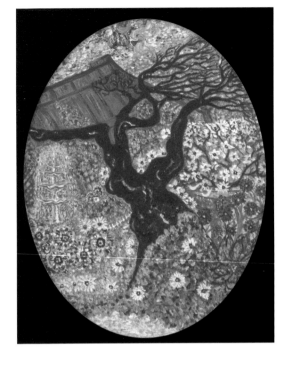

Dead Tree at Pankosmion
1994
Oil on canvas
14 x 11 inches

Gemini Moon
1994
Enamel and metallic gouache on canvas
12 x 9 inches

Taurean Moon
1994
Enamel and metallic gouache on canvas
10 x 8 inches

Edmund's Tree Song
2001
Oil and wax on board
12 x 16 inches

Pregnant with Creation
2007
Oil on canvas
36 x 30 inches

Expressionism

Many of Kleefeld's paintings such as her *Linear Fantasies* and *Lovers* are lyrical and joyous. She has also produced other works that are bracing, bold, and invigorating, conveying a profound and passionate type of energy. As seen in *Reconciliation* (2004), *Shakti* (2004), and *Sheer Nomad* (2003), these paintings have a powerful, arresting tone. Direct and primitive in feel, they can best be characterized by the term *Expressionism*. While they do not constitute a series proper, they do reflect a desire for philosophical, psychological, and spiritual introspection—a vital and recurrent theme in Kleefeld's art.

When Kleefeld approaches a blank canvas, she does not do so with preconceived images in mind. Rather, she prefers to function as a vessel or instrument, open and willing to receive larger forces. Sometimes that energy is positive and light-hearted. At other times, it is distressed, shadowy, and mysterious. When negative messages emerge, Kleefeld feels compelled to accept them honestly and let them appear on her canvas. In fact, allowing the Shadow to emerge can be more instructive, for it often captures truths the conscious mind prefers to hide. She believes that some of her best work comes from the grist, the struggle, the duel of polarities.

Reconciliation (2004) consists of an array of coarse, crude marks spread laterally across the canvas. These symbols seem rudimentary. They are pictograms—raw and direct primal signs that stand somewhere between images and words. With strong linear thrusts, these shapes resemble spears, lances, or arrows—implements that cut and pierce. Tough tools are required to penetrate deep within the psyche.

What lies in the unconscious is often rough and unrefined. Art historian Ernst Gombrich once noted that "Freud's dream symbols are also enigmatic, monstrous and opaque."[1] Kleefeld's expressive language has similar qualities; what is found in the recess of the unconscious mind is often shapeless, embryonic, and amorphous. These coarse symbols tend to be harshly exaggerated or crudely simplistic since primal emotions lack the refinement of social conditioning. As seen in *Reconciliation* (2004), the linear marks can be seen as weapons but also as lines of verification. The material of the psyche has broken down, been laid bare, and then resolved on a higher plane. Reconciling or balancing polarities is a prevalent and crucial theme in Kleefeld's art.

Shakti (2004) is a light and bright painting featuring a sumptuous and potent field of glowing yellow. The title refers to the Hindu personification of the divine feminine. In India, Shakti is revered as the most important of female goddesses. She is a multi-dimensional deity, known and worshipped under different names, with various characteristics and traits. For Kleefeld, Shakti embodies the full range of feminine power, or sacred female energy. The Surrealist artist Max Ernst once wrote, "Painting takes place on two different yet complementary levels. It provides aggressiveness and exaltation."[2] Kleefeld offers interpretations of these forces in *Shakti,* which combines opposing themes of primal strength and joyous celebration.

Painting provides Kleefeld with the means to express the many facets of her complex nature. By working through divergent energies and sublimated instincts, the individual can externalize and release such

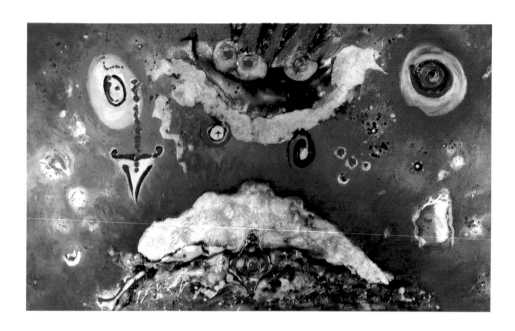

Shakti
2004
Mixed media on canvas
36 x 60 inches

Reconciliation
2004
Mixed media on canvas
36 x 60 inches

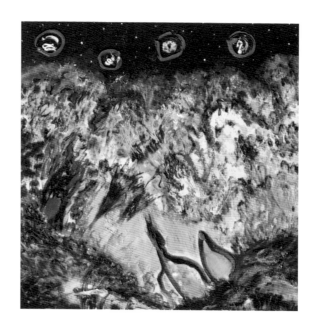

Sheer Nomad
2003
Oil on canvas
30 x 30 inches

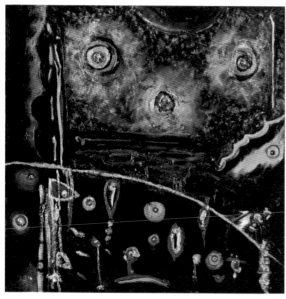

Night Seed Transmission
2007
Oil and acrylic on canvas
30 x 30 inches

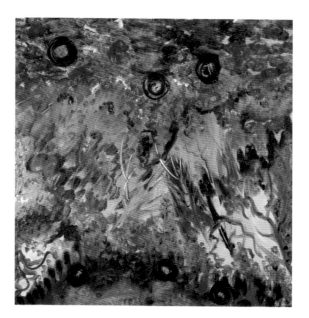

Entities Reflected
2002
Oil on canvas
30 x 30 inches

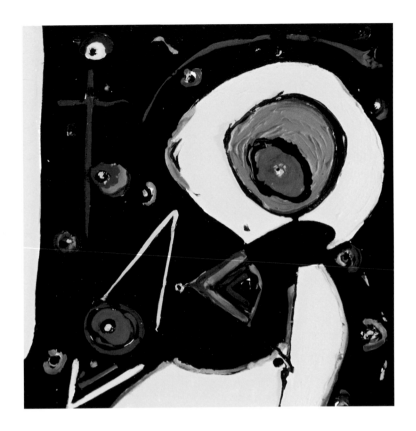

Howling
2004
Mixed media on canvas
30 x 30 inches

Oracle Caves
2003
Oil on canvas
30 x 30 inches

emotions. Expressionism for Kleefeld has a purgative effect. By projecting unsettled conflicts onto the canvas, she can resolve them and herself into an integrated whole.

Sheer Nomad (2003) addresses the idea that artists who probe into the psyche are explorers of the unknown. In a way, they are nomads who wander through uncharted territory. Symbols emerge like beacons that define points of illumination that are encountered along the way. The forms that Kleefeld found and captured were often unexpected and surprising even to her. As the German Expressionist Franz Marc noted, "A symbol arises from a fortuitous impulse."[3] The background of *Sheer Nomad* and many other works is dark, nearly black, and suggests the hidden mysteries that lay in the recesses of the unconscious.

This idea of a journey into dark corners is also captured in *Oracle Caves* (2003). An oracle has been defined as someone or something with wise or prophetic knowledge. The ancient Greeks revered certain sites as possessing these powers. For Kleefeld, this insight comes from deep within the self. As in her canvases referring to grottoes, she employs the cavern to signal psychological depths. When she paints, she functions as an explorer or a voyager into her own psyche, a bold spelunker of the soul.

Henri Matisse once described art as a soothing armchair for a tired businessman, a recipe for complacency. Other times art must shout out in an angry and loud, primal scream. *Howling* (2004) is a naked cry in the wilderness. Kleefeld lives with two Husky dogs that resemble wolves, and she loves and truly identifies with these animals, often revered as totem animals by Native Americans. The title also alludes to the theme of *Howl and Other Poems*, a seminal 1956 book by Kleefeld's friend, the Beat poet Allen Ginsberg, that altered the course of American poetry and culture. It is useful to remember that the word "express" derives from a root meaning "to push out." Expressing involves a forceful ejection. Kleefeld's *Expressionist* paintings are driven by a howling, primal impulse. As she once explained, "Creative expression requires an overflow of energy."[4]

Kleefeld sees this projection of mental energy as akin to sowing seeds, a theme conveyed in *Night Seed Transmission* (2007). "Seed" is among her favorite concepts for it implies beginnings and future growth. She once said, "My visual art reveals the seeds, buds, blossoms, fruits and the pollen of my interplay with the unknown."[5] Philosopher Gaston Bachelard shared this idea, noting that "In times of great discoveries, a poetic image can be the seed of a world, the seed of a universe imagined out of a poet's reverie."[6]

Entities Reflected (2002) features a night sky traversed by a bold band of shimmering red and yellow. Resembling the Milky Way, this belt of light is itself filled with a network of sinuous blood-red lines. These red rivulets look like an aerial view of woodland streams as well as a mammal's circulatory system. Kleefeld views outer space as not empty at all, but rather as organic and expanding, filled with the same pulse of living energy that drives rivers through the hills or blood through our veins. Robinson Jeffers, a poet who shares Kleefeld's pantheistic beliefs, also drew analogies between our bodies and nature, as seen in his line: "Canyon creeks that are my arteries, hair of forest and body of rock."[7]

The colors in the *Expressionist* works tend to emphasize red, yellow, white and black—all hues of primal matter. Yellow is the color of the sand, soil, and earth. Red is the color of clay, blood, and fire. White is the color of light and the spirit. Black is the color of burnt matter and charcoal. In the alchemical tradition, these colors reflect basic psychological states and symbolize the four ancient humors: blood, phlegm, choler, and melancholy. Together these colors form the bedrock of existence, containing the root and energy of life itself.

Kleefeld also produced a series of abstract portraits that draw upon this palette of colors and convey an intensely expressionist vision. *Pregnant with Creation* (2007), rendered in elemental black, white, and red, was inspired by a Picasso exhibition Kleefeld saw at the San Francisco Museum of Modern Art.[8] It depicts an unusual hybrid figure that looks directly at the viewer. It has probing eyes that peer through a visor-like

Dos Bravados
2006
Mixed media on paper
30 x 23 inches

Seated Profiles
2007
Mixed media on paper
12 x 12 inches

opening. With a head that resembles a helmet or antennae, this creature stands alert and ready to receive inspiration from the universe.

The same colors are used in *Seated Profiles* (2007) and in *Dos Bravados* (2006). *Seated Profiles* resembles some works by Picasso, but here Kleefeld uses the image to depict herself as the source of feminine creation. *Dos Bravados* pictures two individuals acting in tandem. Bravados are renegade soldiers. In her painting, Kleefeld paints herself as a bold perpetrator of artistic and psychic adventures.

Horse in Anguish . . . (1994), a highly personal and wonderfully idiosyncratic work, does not resemble other works in this series, but may be considered expressionist simply in terms of the intensity of content. This painting is autobiographical and was made during a highly emotional time in Kleefeld's life. She painted it while her father was dying. The original full title was *Horse in Anguish Holds the Branch of Life and Death Between Its Teeth* and conveys the artist's deep love and concern for her father.

The oval format is intimate and lyrical, harking back to pleasant and well-mannered 18th-century Rococo decorations. This beautiful, genteel surface reveals a deep passion. The horse is worried and is in a state of distress. It is a symbolic self-portrait and alludes to Kleefeld's childhood companion, Mabel. This horse does not run. In fact, it stands frozen in space, immobile, as if it was unable to act. The wide, staring eyes capture a sense of suffering and turmoil. Yet this animal stands resolute, conveying an inner strength. D.H. Lawrence remarked on this quality of horses when he wrote, "The horse is always the symbol of the strong animal life of man."[9] Kleefeld survived the loss of her father and became a stronger person in the process. She knows that to grow, we must face, endure, and ultimately triumph over adversity. To use one of her favorite phrases, it is "grist for the mill," something we must struggle with in order to expand and progress with a deeper and wiser consciousness.

---

1 E. H. Gombrich, "The Use of Art for the Study of Symbols," in James Hogg, ed., *Psychology and the Visual Arts: Selected Readings* (Baltimore: Penguin Books, 1969), 168.

2 Werner Spies, ed., *Max Ernst: A Retrospective* (London, 1991), 9.

3 Franz Marc quoted in Werner Haftmann, *German Art of the Twentieth Century* (New York: The Museum of Modern Art, 1957), 18.

4 "Singing Songs of Ecstasy with Carolyn Mary Kleefeld," in David Jay Brown and Rebecca McClen Novick, *Mavericks of the Mind: Conversations for the New Millennium* (Freedom, CA: The Crossing Press, 1993), 162.

5 *Mavericks of the Mind*, 160.

6 Gaston Bachelard, *The Poetics of Reverie* (Boston: Beacon Press, 1969), 1.

7 Tim Hunt, ed., *The Selected Poetry of Robinson Jeffers* (Stanford: Stanford University Press, 2001), 739.

8 "Picasso and American Art" was shown at the San Francisco Museum of Modern Art from February 23, 2007 through May 28, 2007.

9 D. H. Lawrence, "Etruscan Places," 108.

After Picasso
1995
Oil on canvas
14 x 11 inches

Horse in Anguish . . .
1994
Enamel and gouache on canvas
10 x 8 inches

Izabella, the Polish Gypsy
2007
Oil on canvas
20 x 20 inches

Portraits

Kleefeld has been making magical portraits since she was a child. The little improvisational skits she performed for her mother's friends were based on her imaginary characters, such as those conjured from swirls of floating dust particles in her youthful stories about *The Nanose*. It is clear that from these earliest years, Kleefeld was fascinated by personalities. This interest led to her adult concern with psychology and with exploring the human mind. She considers many of the paintings discussed earlier in this essay to be portraits, but most observers would probably not recognize them as such. For example, many of her earliest works, such as *Cleo*, *Tree Face of Metamorphosis*, and *Un-Dryad* are portraits. But they do not imitate a physical form. They are portraits of a soul, renderings of an inner being.

A portrait is defined as an image that represents a specific person, a likeness that captures an individual's unique features. But what exactly constitutes a "likeness?" Most people might cite visual resemblance, but this is superficial. Human beings are far more complex. Each person is made of a vast array of factors too broad to be reduced to a simple mirror image. The most telling part of an individual's being—the personality—has, in fact, no immediate visual form.

In 2007, Kleefeld embarked on a new series of spiritual portraits. They depict various people in her life. Most follow a similar size and format—a 20-by-20-inch square. This scale allows her to produce an image commensurate with the actual size of a person's face. The titles—*Flowering Enthusiasm, Mauve with Perception* and *Captain Voodoo*—offer no clue as to who is represented. But those who are familiar with these members of the Big Sur community may easily connect an image with a name. In fact, despite the lack of visual correspondences, these portraits successfully capture the essence of each person in a manner that can be quite accurate and revealing.

These poetic, symbolic paintings capture personalities by using an assortment of discrete symbols. Forms are for the most part well-defined with sharp boundaries, distinct color areas, and clear linear outlines. Color is vivid and bright. The attention paid to the formal components infuses the paintings with a visual power and pictorial strength.

Kleefeld was inspired to produce this series after seeing an exhibition at the Norton Simon Museum of Art in Pasadena devoted to the Expressionist painter, Alexei Jawlensky.[1] Jawlensky was a Russian and a pioneering modernist, who participated in the explosion of avant-garde art in the first decades of the 20th century. He played a role in development of abstract painting by his friend and colleague, Vassily Kandinsky, who was another of Kleefeld's muses. Portraits represent a large part of his production. After 1905, he discovered the art of the French Fauves and adopted their techniques to produce boldly expressive portraits featuring schematized forms, flat areas of color, and heavy black outlines. He was also interested in the spiritual dimension of art and explored metaphysical movements such as Theosophy and mysticism. His best known works are his late abstract portraits—*Mystical Heads* (1917-19) and *Savior's Faces* (1918-21)—where he used the human visage to convey a higher, transcendent meaning.

Jawlensky successfully blended the decorative qualities of Matisse and the French Fauves with a deep and fundamental sense of native religiosity. One perceptive writer noted that he combined "the strong colors and bold outlines of the Fauves" with "influences from the Russian traditions of icon painting and peasant art to form a highly personal style that expressed his passionate temperament and mystical conception of art. A mood of melancholy introspection—far removed from the ebullience of Fauvism—is characteristic of much of his work and it has been said that he 'saw Matisse through Russian eyes.'"[2]

As a soulful Russian, Jawlensky was able to temper the prettiness of Fauvist art and give it a Slavic poignancy. In the translation from one cultural perspective to another, the work gained in substance and resonance. Kleefeld, who is also of Russian ancestry, was drawn to this sense of gravitas. She prizes soulfulness and in the introspective Jawlensky found a kindred spirit. He became another of her muses—an individual of rare poetic and artistic vision who serves as a beacon for her own art.

Although Kleefeld was moved by Jawlensky's portraits, her paintings do not resemble his work. She began with a general idea of an intensified, abstract image but formulated it in her own way. If there is any one feature unifying her portrait series, it is constant inventiveness. Rather than develop a single image or style and use it for different people, she approaches each composition afresh, starting with the aura of a specific person. The distinct mix of traits, quirks, and characteristics arising from the essence of each subject guides her technique. As a result, these paintings are dissimilar and dramatically innovative.

For example Feral Creature, which depicts a wild, untamed persona, was rendered in a loose, ad hoc, expressionist manner. While painting the face, Kleefeld applied flowing areas of color that freely merge and blend. Around the chaotic frenzy of the face, she added a solid field of brilliant red. The background is more orderly and resolved than the figure, making a decisive comment on the unpredictable and aggressive nature of the subject. In contrast, the forms in Noah, the Guardian are all clear and resolved. Each area of color is solid and distinct. The black lines defining the figure are certain and true and portray a person who is stolid and sure—a steady, dependable protector.

These portraits depict each subject's psyche, and all together, they offer a kaleidoscope of personality types, running the full gamut of human nature. Flowering Enthusiasm is joyous and upbeat, depicting someone who overflows with an abundant sense of the world's endless possibilities. In Mauve with Perception, the viewer encounters a shy, contemplative soul, one who lives a rich inner life. Captain Voodoo pictures a wise healer, one who is a master of great and powerful forces. Izabella, the Polish Gypsy discloses an eternal wanderer, with incisive, probing, electric eyes.

Kleefeld's desire to delve into the essence of a person reflects her deeply poetic sensibility. It is a perspective she shares with sensitive writers such as Henry Miller. Once, Miller explained what it was like for him to paint his friend, California artist Hilaire Hiler,

> The first glance tells you that you are in the presence of an artist. There is something amiss—at once. Another victim of life. Another sufferer. Another tragic figure. This is all under the surface, however— what one feels, not what one sees with the eyes. Superficially one sees a pleasant, good-natured, slightly gruff individual.[3]

His explanation could be a description of one of Kleefeld's portraits. Both Kleefeld and Miller see life as too rich and wondrous to ever accept simple, superficial appearances. Both are too inquisitive to be satisfied with imitation, which they reject as monotonous and dreary. But delving into the character behind a person's public face requires a greater involvement and commitment on the part of the artist. To truly see another's soul, one must possess the bravery to look deeply into one's own soul. Both Kleefeld and Miller have this type of poetic insight and artistic courage.

Mauve with Perception
2007
Oil on canvas
20 x 20 inches

Monsieur Bobcat
2007
Oil on canvas
20 x 20 inches

Michael the Magician
2008
Oil on canvas
20 x 20 inches

Moon Eyes
2007
Oil on canvas
20 x 20 inches

Feral Business
2005
Oil on canvas
20 x 20inches

Eclipse of the Heart
2007
Oil on canvas
20 x 20 inches

Feral Creature
2007
Oil on canvas
20 x 20 inches

Evocation of Dylan Thomas
2007
Oil on canvas
20 x 20 inches

Flowering Enthusiasm
2007
Oil on canvas
20 x 20 inches

1   The exhibition *Alexei Jawlensky (1864-1941)* was shown at the Norton Simon Museum of Art from May 4 to November 5, 2007.
    In another curious example of synchronicity, Frederick Weisman, founder of the Frederick R. Weisman Museum of Art which
    organized this exhibition of art by Carolyn Kleefeld, was the brother-in-law of Norton Simon.

2   Ian Chilvers, ed., *The Oxford Dictionary of Art* (New York: Oxford University Press, 2004), 363.

3   Henry Miller, "A Letter," in Hilaire Hiler, Henry Miller and William Saroyan, *Why Abstract?* (London: The Falcon Press, Ltd., 1948), 38.

Noah, the Guardian
2007
Oil on canvas
20 x 20 inches

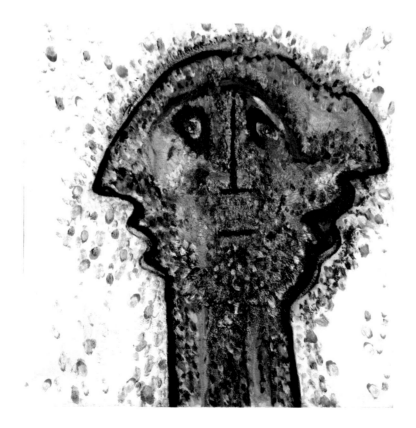

Paradox of Profiles
2007
Oil on canvas
20 x 20 inches

The Poet
2007
Oil on canvas
20 x 20 inches

Seeking Salvation
2007
Oil on canvas
20 x 20 inches

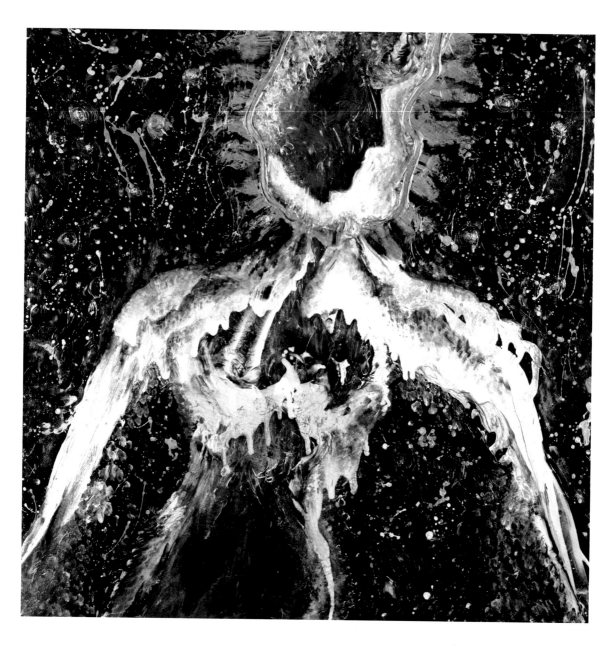

Laura Huxley's Departure
2007
Acrylic on canvas
48 x 48 inches

Laura Archera Huxley

Carolyn Kleefeld met Laura Huxley, the widow of Aldous Huxley in the late 1980s.[1] That fortuitous meeting blossomed into a long friendship that lasted until Laura's death on December 13, 2007 at the age of 96. The two women shared a rich relationship, and over the years Laura wrote insightful forewords to Kleefeld's books, *The Alchemy of Possibility* (1998) and *Soul Seeds* (2008), as well as moving testimonials for her other books.[2]

Laura Archera Huxley was a musician, author, freelance filmmaker, and lay psychotherapist, and she is perhaps best remembered for her humanitarian work with children. Born in Italy in 1911, she studied violin, became a musical prodigy, and made her United States debut in 1937 at Carnegie Hall. She met Aldous Huxley in 1948 when she approached him to make a documentary film. They married in 1956. In 1963, she wrote a self-help book, *You Are Not the Target*. After Aldous died that year—on the same day as President John F. Kennedy—Laura devoted her life to maintaining his works and reputation. Adopting her young granddaughter, Karen Pfeiffer, in the 1970s gave her an additional focus working with youth. In 1978, she founded the nonprofit group *Children: Our Ultimate Investment*, a foundation concerned with the education and parenting of young people. She saw children as best representing her husband's belief in the "human potential."

Kleefeld shared Laura Huxley's bold, impassioned, loving, and creative approach to life. Although Laura had grown blind in her last years, this impairment did little to slow her enthusiasm or will to experience life to the fullest. Kleefeld would make bimonthly trips to Los Angeles to visit Laura, during which Carolyn would read her poetry and the two would spontaneously voyage together on many a philosophical journey. These trips continued through Laura's final illness and death, when Carolyn was at Laura's side.

Kleefeld was moved by losing her dear friend and muse, and was inspired to honor her in this group of paintings, along with many poems written over the years.[3] It is fitting that these paintings depict her passing and the ultimate reunion of her spirit with that of her husband. Laura Huxley believed in the importance of change and embraced periods of transition as opportunities to realize new possibilities. This is how she approached death. In *This Timeless Moment*, her 1968 memoir of her life with Aldous, Laura wrote that we can approach death in two different ways:

> There are two diametrically opposite views about dying. One is that the best way is to go without knowing it, to slip away—hopefully when sleeping. The other view—less prevalent but more spiritually enlightened—is that one should die as aware and clear-minded as possible; that death is one of the great adventures of life, and one should not miss it or block it by unconsciousness. In this view, it is thought that the future life of the "soul" or "consciousness" or "mind" (whatever word one uses for that which pervades the body and gives it life) is influenced to a great extent by the thoughts and feelings at the moment of death.[4]

She and Aldous firmly believed in the second approach for it allowed one to fully experience this last transition.

The Eleventh Hour
2007
Acrylic on canvas
20 x 20 inches

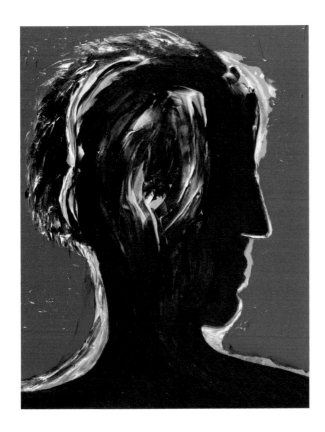

Reunion of Aldous and Laura
2007
Acrylic on board
14 x 18 inches

Reunion of Laura and Aldous
2007
Acrylic on board
14 x 18 inches

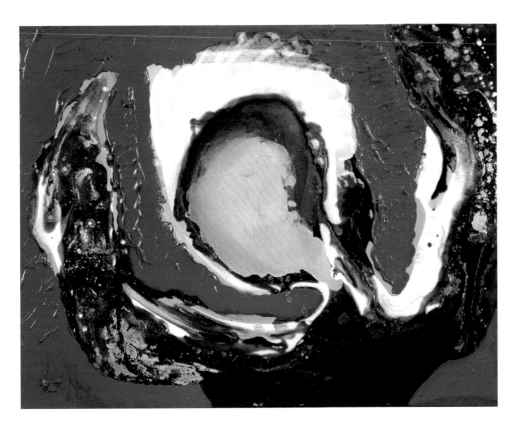

Kleefeld's poignant paintings celebrate Laura's death as a grand passage. *The Eleventh Hour* (2007) depicts Laura in her last days. Although her body had weakened, her spirit was still powerful. *Laura Huxley's Departure* (2007) shows her soul leaving the earth and about to partake in a marvelous adventure. *Reunion of Aldous and Laura* (2007) and *Reunion of Laura and Aldous* (2007) show the glorious meeting of two souls.

The images of Laura Huxley are almost all black. Modern artists beginning with Manet have used this color to resolve artistic dilemmas. But Kleefeld's focus was less on a pictorial problem and more on a spiritual one. In western culture, black is the traditional color associated with death and mourning. But for Kleefeld, this color has a rich symbolism beyond social custom. She adheres to Carl Jung's belief that black is a potent and primal sign of transformation. Jung identified darkening or blackening as the first and essential stage of an alchemical process advancing towards a higher and more complete state. Black also has more colors in it than any other, symbolizing to Kleefeld the multiple experiences essential to the psychic process of death and rebirth.

Blackness also signals spiritual depth. In the last years of his life, Alexei Jawlensky, an artist Kleefeld admires, focused on a series of highly abstract heads. Known as the *Meditations*, these reductive, minimal faces sought to capture the essence of the human presence and soul. Many consist simply of a few straight lines, demarcating brow, nose, and mouth, inscribed into a black ground. As Jawlensky explained, "In my last works I have taken away the magic of color in order to concentrate on nothing but spiritual depth."[5] In her *Laura Huxley* series, Kleefeld used black to indicate the depth of this great and compassionate woman.

---

1   The event was a meeting of the Albert Hoffman Foundation in Hollywood. Ram Dass, Andrew Weil, and others were also in attendance.

2   In Laura Huxley's foreword to Carolyn Kleefeld, *Soul Seeds: Revelations and Drawings*, she wrote: "Let yourself be enchanted by these evanescent images, varying flights in the immensity of the Universe . . ."

3   One of Kleefeld's poems, "Being Silence," written to commemorate Aldous, was read at the opening of the Fourth International Aldous Huxley Symposium at the Huntington Library in San Marino, California, July 30–August 3, 2008.

4   Laura Archera Huxley, *This Timeless Moment: a Personal View of Aldous Huxley* (New York: Farrar, Straus & Giroux, 1968), 262.

5   James Demetrion, *Alexei Jawlensky: a Centennial Exhibition* (Pasadena: Pasadena Art Museum, 1964), 63.

Carolyn Kleefeld and Laura Archera Huxley, 1998

Pink Creature
2008
Colored and metallic pens on paper
8.5 x 5 inches

Conclusion—Fire and Renewal

In the early summer of 2008 Carolyn Kleefeld commenced work on a new painting of a standing female figure. As it progressed, the figure took on a certain resonance and majesty. Eventually it would be titled *Priestess of Dawn*. Wearing a crown resembling feathers and flames, this stately and noble woman projects a regal and distinctly feminine aura. But the completion of this canvas would be postponed by events beyond human control. Eventually, the image was destined to serve as a symbol of survival and renewal.

As the work neared completion, a front of powerful, unseasonable thunderstorms moved onshore. Heavy lightning strikes ignited bone-dry forests, and by the end of June, over 1,000 fires were burning throughout northern and central California. Starting on June 21 and continuing through mid-July, the Basin Complex Fire threatened homes and businesses over large areas of the Big Sur coast.

Fire-fighting helicopters flew directly over Kleefeld's house to skylift water from the sea below her home. As the flames approached nearby her home, a team of friends joined together to wrap and transport the paintings—including all that are in this exhibition—to safety in Monterey. Kleefeld's home and the others in proximity were spared. By the time the fire was fully contained on July 27, the Basin Complex Fire had burned 162,818 acres and destroyed over fifty structures. Returning after the evacuation, Kleefeld surveyed acres of burnt forest and observed that the environs resembled "a crematorium." The gathering of friends and community to support one another in meeting the challenges of this emergency inspired in Kleefeld and in many others a renewed faith in the human spirit.

As one might expect, Kleefeld responded to the fire through her art. She produced many drawings, such as *Big Sur's Fire Face* that recall the anxiety of those weeks when Big Sur was imperiled. These works are part of a larger group which may be called *Automatic Drawings*. Such works, as Kleefeld has produced for decades, form an essential component of her artistic practice.

Her numerous *Automatic Drawings* are rendered with various pens and colored markers that allow her to work quickly, which is essential to her method. The term "automatism" was introduced by Andre Breton, the founder of Surrealism, who conceived of the procedure as a way to access unconscious thoughts. In the first Manifesto of Surrealism of 1924, he defined the technique:

> SURREALISM, *n*. Psychic automatism in its pure state, by which one proposes to express—verbally, by means of the written word, or in any other manner—the actual functioning of thought. Dictated by thought, in the absence of any control exercised by reason, exempt from any aesthetic or moral concern.[1]

Breton believed that centuries of western rationality had dulled both the mind and senses. The practice of automatism as a liberating force could free the individual from stifling inhibitions and the mental baggage of social conditioning. The goal is to use the hand to write or draw quickly and spontaneously and thus to outpace the rational mind's critical faculties. Free from conscious control, the resulting images convey an immediate energy that is fresh and revealing, along with a sense of the magical that Breton called "the marvelous."

Myriad Poseurs
2008
Colored pens on paper
12 x 9 inches

She Questions the Contradictions
2008
Colored and metallic pens on paper
11 x 14.75 inches

Evacuation (Fire Series)
2008
Colored pens on paper
11.75 x 11.75 inches

Discombobulation (Fire Series)
2008
Colored and fluorescent pens on paper
11.75 x 11.75 inches

Big Sur's Fire Face (Fire Series)
2008
Colored pens on paper
11.75 x 11.75 inches

House of the Neither-Nor Realm (Fire Series)
2008
Colored and metallic pens on paper
11.75 x 11.75 inches

Like Breton, Kleefeld experiences the process of working from deep within the psyche as unbounded and yielding of art which is innovative and genuine. She sometimes works on her drawings while engaged in another activity, such as talking on the phone. With her attention distracted, she is able to let her hand roam freely, responding to rhythms not governed by conscious thought. The images are ornate and complex. Forms are self-generative, as one set of marks instinctively leads to another. Shapes beget shapes; patterns produce patterns in a rich and provocative tapestry. Forms rage, push, and propel their way across the paper in an explosion of creative energy. Kleefeld has produced drawings in this manner for decades.

It is worth noting that a good majority of Kleefeld's automatic drawings are abstract figures. These personages stand vertical and appear like totems, harbingers of another race. They are like us but are strange and unfamiliar. They are denizens of the mind, inhabitants of an inner, psychic realm. They also reflect Kleefeld's deep conviction that we are all creatures of one creation. In fact, in everyday speech the term "creature" refers to a generic category of living beings. Kleefeld uses the word as a term of endearment. She refers to her closest friends as "Creech," a shortened form of "creature." In her world and art, we are all creatures of the universe, sharing an interwoven fate.

Although some of the drawings made during the fire seem disturbed and defensive—a response to the furies—many are whimsical, even humorous. The joy of each derives from the wonder of the creative act. Kleefeld revels in the miraculous quality of these magical, fantastic beings. Like beloved friends with charming flaws, these creatures are magnificently idiosyncratic and evoke our common humanity.

After the fire, Kleefeld returned to *Priestess of Dawn*, as one would revisit an old friend. Much had occurred in the days they had been apart. In a few short weeks, the lives of friends and neighbors who lost homes had been abruptly transformed. The artist picked up her brush and continued her dialogue with the *Priestess*. The resulting image glows with a radiant light. By using iridescent pigment, Kleefeld is able to convey an inner glow. Like the artist herself, *Priestess of Dawn* survived the fire and remains "governed by the ancient rhythms," the original title of this painting. In her art, Kleefeld invites us all to join in attunement with these rhythms and thus to emerge inspired to venture onward, together and each with our own creative journey.

---

1   Andre Breton, *Manifestoes of Surrealism* (Ann Arbor: University of Michigan Press, 1972), 26

Priestess of Dawn
2008
Acrylic and ink on canvas
60 x 48 inches

Acknowledgements

Numerous individuals have contributed to the success of this exhibition and catalog. Above all, I wish to express my sincere thanks to the artist, Carolyn Mary Kleefeld. She opened her art and home to me and gave much of her personal time. Allowing the Frederick R. Weisman Museum of Art and me the opportunity to present her paintings to the public is a sign of her faith in my vision. For that trust, I am deeply grateful.

In Big Sur, Carolyn has many close friends, who are also her colleagues, assisting her with her numerous art, writing and creative projects. I have named them—with great affection—the Carolingians. They all contributed to this exhibition and have earned my earnest appreciation. Linda Parker, marketing manager, was my first guide to Big Sur and to Carolyn's studio. Patricia Holt, one of the artist's closest friends, provided astute editorial skills and profound wisdom every step of the way. Both Linda and Patricia were essential and they have my heartfelt gratitude. Laura Zabrowski serves admirably as the artist's personal assistant. Kirtana is a long-time editor. Ronna Emmons is an art consultant. Sarah Staples and Natalie Van Allen maintain archives and databases; Gail Bengard and Cathy Jaeger framed works in the exhibition.

I want to thank John Dotson, who provided his editing skills for this publication and Kodiak Greenwood, who photographed many of the images in this book. John Larson took some of the photographs of Carolyn Kleefeld.

I would also like to acknowledge the many friends and neighbors who assisted in a myriad of tasks, including packing and evacuating the art for this exhibition during the Great Basin Fire of late June and July 2008, including many of the people above, as well as David Dunn, Marla Bell, Nicki Ehrlich, John Larson, David Mendez, Scott Parker, Vickers, Luke Zabrowski, Josh Zabrowski.

At Pepperdine University I am grateful to the assistance given by my friends and colleagues at the Center for the Arts, including Rebecca Carson, Managing Director; Erin Harris, Administrative Assistant; and Brad White, Publicity Manager. I am especially appreciative of the tireless energy and support of Carol Kmiec, Museum Assistant and Arts Education Coordinator.

The creative vision and professional skill of the University Communications team resulted in this exhibition catalog. I wish to thank Brett Sizemore, Director of Creative Services for his leadership; Gayle Wheatley, Art Director for the beautiful design of this publication, and Jill McWilliams, Production Manager, for handling the myriad logistics of producing this publication.

Michael Zakian, Director
Frederick R. Weisman Museum of Art